Holistic Indoor Gardening

A Panoptic View Through the Lens of Earthship Greenhouse Management

Written and Illustrated by

Daniel Dynan

Edited
by Helen Rynaski

CONTENTS

The dedication of this book is to my wonderful wife, without whom I would not have had the time, confidence, and courage to attempt a project of this size. I am humbly grateful and always appreciative of all that you contribute in my life. You are the greatest blessing, and I love you.

PREFACE

I remember the first time I visited the Earthship community in Taos, New Mexico. I was on a short road trip from southern Colorado to Albuquerque for a workshop. I had never heard of Earthships at all, but a handful of friends told me that if I was going through Taos, I had to stop and see them. I thought it was maybe some crazy art installation in the desert where people carved pirate ships out of the mountainside, which wasn't that far off, now that I think about it. I ended up going to the Earthship Biotecture Visitor Center and taking a short tour of the building they had open at the time. I thought to myself, as I was going through the premises, if all the claims of being able to live off-grid by designing the home this way were true, why was this not more widespread?

When the tour was over, there was someone on staff you could speak to about any questions that may have come up. I asked some probing ones, without being rude, because I was skeptical about the whole thing, but still profoundly interested and maybe slightly perplexed. As I stood there at the end of the tour digesting all this information, I saw a planter bed and, in it, a six-foot banana plant flowering with maybe fifty bananas on it. It felt like it was staring me in the face. I had never seen anything like that in my life and was stunned that there was a tropical fruit thriving in a high desert environment. Everything I had just experienced stuck with me for the rest of my trip.

I needed some time to mull it over. When I got home, I researched Earthships extensively. This led me to apply for an internship on-site and, in turn, to my employment with the company and, ultimately, to working with the plants in the greenhouses and teaching the academy course. In a way, I feel indebted to that banana tree because, without it, I probably wouldn't be living the life that I feel so blessed to have.

I met my wife, Ashley, while working at Earthship Biotecture. Since our wedding in 2016, we have done a lot of traveling and worked and volunteered on many organic farms throughout Europe and United States. We have also taken numerous courses which increased our knowledge of holistic farming practices, as we are passionate about whole foods and earth stewardship.

At the end of our travel phase, in late 2018, we returned to Taos to put roots down and begin settling in. I began teaching horticulture classes at Earthship Biotecture Academy. The students that the academy draws are an eclectic mix. Some are advanced permaculture enthusiasts, others proficient builders looking to expand their repertoire, and many are just beginning their journey into the world of sustainability. During my time as an employee, and now as a consultant for Earthship Biotecture, I have always noted, about the groups who come to study here, there is a genuine hunger for more in-depth knowledge of the methods behind managing an Earthship greenhouse. Until now, there have only been bits and pieces of information that those interested could attempt to piece together to gain some understanding, but nothing presented the whole spectrum of greenhouse management and tied loose ends together in one place.

The creation of this book spawned from my desire to serve the Earthship students better. There is not enough class time to provide a full in-depth look into all aspects involved in running a holistic Earthship greenhouse. There are always more questions than time to answer them from friends, colleagues, and students alike. That is why I took the opportunity to distill and consolidate all the diverse aspects of operating an Earthship greenhouse into one synthesized and easy-to-understand guide. My sincere hope is that this book will reinforce and further strengthen those of you already adept in the sustainability field, as well as act as an open doorway on the path to living a holistic life for those of you who may be new to these types of methodologies. I have a real heart and passion for the Earthship mission, and I wish the readers all the best in their future endeavors.

INTRODUCTION

Earthships are a form of autonomous and sustainable housing created by Michael Reynolds. There are six design principles to Earthship construction. The principles are building with natural and recycled materials, thermal/solar heating and cooling, solar and wind electricity, water harvesting, contained sewage treatment, and food production. *Holistic Indoor Gardening* is a long-overdue comprehensive look into the last design principle of food production. Since the inception of Earthship educational programs, students have been calling out for a definitive manual on this topic. This book is an attempt to consolidate and clearly outline all the varied aspects involved in holistic greenhouse management. While the inspiration for this book comes from hands-on experience working in Earthship structures, the content and practices apply to far more than just Earthship greenhouses, and it illuminates a unique method of indoor gardening.

The organizational structure of this book is designed to equip the reader step by step with a set of practical tools and knowledge for interfacing with a greenhouse in a holistic fashion. It is also intended to provide a window into the methods and techniques that have proven effective for Earthship greenhouse management. The material is designed to provide useful takeaways to a broad spectrum of people. It contains some technical and advanced concepts, as well as fundamental and elementary ones. The format is designed to be helpful to both the advanced greenhouse manager in casting a vision for possible future improvements and the novice greenhouse manager in warding off any potential pitfalls.

There are differing philosophies of design and management in working with an in-home greenhouse. Each view will have a degree of suitability for the individual's interests, lifestyle, and skill level. Implementing and running a program that is as holistic as possible within the greenhouse space is the primary thrust of this book. Therefore, it is focused on maximizing yields and beneficial interactions, while maintaining a healthy and high-performing overall system. There are notes and references, where appropriate, on alternative management styles that some may choose to practice, but the core of the content will showcase holistic, integrated principles. The principles and practices outlined in this book apply to any greenhouse that fits within the realm of home or residential usage, although some alterations may need to be made, depending on the style and orientation of a particular structure. Also, please note that all diagrams and calculations are for the Northern Hemisphere, so adjust accordingly should you be at a different latitude.

Earthship greenhouse management is specialized, due to the unique conditions that arise in this type of greenhouse. They are multifaceted in their design and function. They are unique in the world today in that very few residential structures incorporate a conservatory as a fundamental element, let alone a greenhouse that can process and utilize greywater. As such, the approach towards the management itself needs to balance a different set of concerns than that of, say, a commercial greenhouse or even a small hobby greenhouse. An Earthship greenhouse is a place in which one both lives and works. In a sense, the building is a living organism, and you are an integral component. It is a place that contributes to the aesthetics of the home. It aids in air purification and provides food and medicine. It functions as a primary source of heating within the structure, and it can significantly assist in the responsible stewardship of water, which is so critical in this day and age. The need for balancing the elements of living, working, and maintaining proper home functions are what make Earthships dynamic and distinctive. The experiences gained from working under these conditions are what make this book stand out from one based strictly on greenhouse management.

A greenhouse is inherently separate from the full complexity and interplay of natural ecosystem forces. Therefore, the individual is responsible for filling in the gaps to the best of their ability. Not every single niche in nature can be included in the greenhouse. In this methodology, a high premium is placed on biomimicry, whenever feasible. Mimicking the patterns of nature within the greenhouse, when most suitable, is important to best uphold total system health and functioning. No greenhouse system will be a hands-off utopia. The greenhouse is continually changing over time. Much effort and astute observation are needed to maintain a harmonious and productive holistic greenhouse.

CHAPTER I

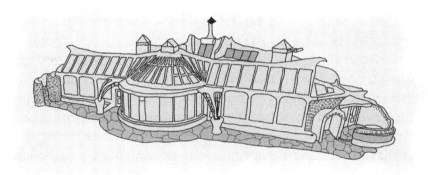

GREENHOUSE STYLES

Over the years, Earthships have undergone many evolutions, upgrades, and modifications, improving upon past shortcomings and striving for maximum autonomous performance. Greenhouse style is the best starting point because the layout and design have a profound effect on reaching the garden's full potential. It is essential to know that extenuating landscape or building requirements dictate any number of different layouts. The drawings and explanations are used to illustrate a typical representation of each greenhouse type, and are by no means a complete list of what you will find out there in the world. This chapter focuses on the interplay of the greenhouse and interior planter layouts and how this impacts performance. Every project will have numerous considerations, so mastering this will help the greenhouse manager reach the best possible outcome. Each greenhouse style and planter orientation comes with particular strengths and weaknesses.

If you are building a new structure, retrofitting an old one, or looking for a better understanding of the one you have, examine the various evolutions in each section. Compare the construction types, in conjunction with the profile on standard planter layouts, and see what may be best suited for your climate, needs, and goals. Also, take note of the challenges each one can present. All of the Earthship models and greenhouse styles in this chapter are buildings that I have either lived in or worked with extensively. Therefore, I have firsthand knowledge of each style's strengths and potential pitfalls.

Across the board, for any style greenhouse, the better the

quality and clarity of the glass installed, the better the performance. Tinted glass, heavy-duty plastic sheets, or plexiglass panels will all add an extra design challenge down the road due to plant temperaments, needs, and sensitivities. Besides, when the home is closed up more consistently (such as in winter), these cheaper options can cause significant condensation. Prolonged exposure to interior condensation can compromise the wood framing and cause mold issues. It is advisable for anyone serious about maintaining a genuinely healthy greenhouse environment to not skimp on the type of glass installed during initial construction. If you do not have access to or cannot afford higher-end glass, do not let that discourage you from trying to build a healthy greenhouse system. Patience, persistence, and research are a big part of success in this area. Many plants will thrive in filtered light or can deal with more significant temperature fluctuations due to material selection. Over time, one can also breed and acclimatize the plants to the unique conditions of a specific greenhouse.

Before we jump into examining each style, I would like to point out that any greenhouse outlined here could have overhead grow lights installed to make up for any gaps in daylight hours, depending on the stage of plant growth or overall greenhouse design. I do not incorporate that aspect in each subsection here, as it is valuable to understand the passive baseline greenhouse performance without added energy inputs. Being as low-tech as possible in design and function, while integrating and harmoniously encountering the forces of the natural world, is a worthy goal. For those of you who may see the incorporation of indoor grow lights as a viable or appealing option, by all means, include it in your design and management process.

MODULAR SINGLE GREENHOUSE

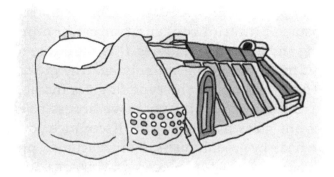

The road to an authentic, autonomous off-grid building was a long and gradual process of experimentation with sustainable techniques. Add a dose of inspired creativity, possibly even some luck and divine intervention, and the first Earthship was born in 1979. It is located in Taos, New Mexico, and is aptly named the Hobbit House. While the drawing at the start of this section is not of that particular building, it shares what all the original Earthships have in common—it is a "modular" design. This style found pre-eminence in the late 1980s to early 1990s. Speckled across all of Taos County are these very artistic and funky homes. While the newer models have a fantastic appeal and many significant performance enhancements, there is something extraordinary about the homes made during the first era of Earthships. They capture a special place in my heart. There must have been something in the air back then. Each one is just brimming with an aura of individuality and love. All the finishes and the energy of the space itself makes one feel alive. If you ever get the chance to visit northern New Mexico, make sure to find time to see an old Modular Earthship. Reading or hearing about them and seeing pictures does not do them just-ice.

A basic mechanism of all Earthships is to use the green-house to maximize solar gain in the winter and minimize solar gain in the summer. Integrated home greenhouses regulate in-terior temperature naturally. Earlier design models, such as this and the Package design (described in the following section), have more significant temperature fluctuations in the home and greenhouse due to only having a single greenhouse.

During this era of construction, when Modular models were at their peak, a lot of excavation was done to establish the interior spaces of the home. This practice still occurs, depend-ing on the landscape, but it is rare due to the risk of flooding the house. Nearly every Modular design includes sloped glass for its exterior greenhouse because of the excavation. If the glass panes are installed vertically instead of at an angle, it will not allow enough solar gain to penetrate deeply enough into the home to charge the thermal mass and maintain a comfort-able living temperature, because the living space is below the natural grade of the property. The following drawings illustrate two typical planter orientations.

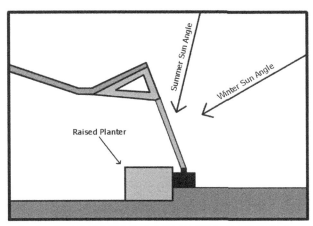

An elevation cut of a Modular greenhouse with a raised bed planter.

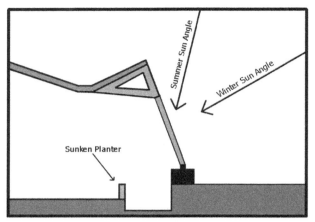

An elevation cut of a Modular greenhouse with a sunken planter.

The first planter option we will look at is one using a raised bed (see the first of the two drawings). I do not recommend this unless, for some reason, the interior makes it necessary—the inability to excavate in the planter area, the designation of the space for an alternate use other than gardening, or the cost. One major pitfall is that a raised bed significantly reduces the overall headroom of your plants. What typically happens is that the plants grow up and make contact with the glass and continue to grow, getting squished up awkwardly, and then burned by the sun. This pattern eventually leads to an early demise of any plant that gets more than a couple of feet tall. A second major pitfall is the squandering of gravity-fed fresh water or greywater. The more pumps added into a system, the more complicated and prone to failure it becomes. The more a greywater system can operate passively and independently of pumps or human interaction, the safer and more hygienic your environment will remain. More details about greywater mechanics and guidelines, which will make it even more clear why it is not recommended to use raised planters in this style, are in a later chapter.

The second option is a sunken planter (see the second of

the two drawings). In my experience, this is the best choice for a Modular design Earthship. You maximize your total grow space and allow larger plants the room to reach maturity and remain healthy and happy. Also, a sunken planter does not squander opportunities to gravity feed, but creates more. This is a real blessing, as we will discuss later.

PACKAGE SINGLE GREENHOUSE

The next step in the evolution of Earthship design was the Package model. Several modifications and alterations make their appearance in this model, but the one most pertinent to the aim of this book is the introduction of vertical glass for the greenhouse. Many do-it-yourself homebuilders opt to build a riff on this style because of its relative ease and simplicity to construct, as well as its overall reliable off-grid performance.

While being the most straightforward to build, this style of Earthship adds a challenging dimension. A single greenhouse of solely vertical glass causes a subtle but significant alteration to the natural course and characteristics of the seasons. Of course, greenhouses in general, are designed to alter and extend seasons, but in the Package design, there is a much more pro-nounced effect. At first glance, one may not notice or think of it, but if you track the solar aspect throughout the year, you will find that summer is not summer at all in the Package Green-house. The same is observable for each season.

Let me illustrate. Let's say it is June 21st, the summer solstice—the day of the year with the most sunlight hours. In a regular outdoor garden, summer crops are in full swing with the maximum amount of daylight hours as well as warmer temperatures. However, in the Package Earthship, unless the structure has large eastern and western windows aligned to the greenhouse, there will be nearly zero direct sun rays hitting your planter the entire day, regardless of whether you opt to install a raised planter or a sunken one (see drawings). The roof will have deflected almost all of the direct rays, and, while the light of the day illuminates the greenhouse, the plants do not behave like they would if they were outside. So, here we see that summer becomes a sort of warm stasis period in the greenhouse instead of the traditional time of rampant growth.

All the other greenhouse styles highlighted in this chapter are uniform in their seasonal periods. They buffer the extremes of spring, summer, and fall, while removing a real winter from the equation. The Package greenhouse, however, creates two "microsummers" in the planter during the couple of weeks approaching and receding from the spring and fall equinoxes. Having summer split into two sections is less than ideal for the plants, because of their genetic and metabolic attunement to the regular rhythm of the seasons. The alteration or disruption of this can cause plants to become stressed and decline in health.

To combat this challenge, the greenhouse manager must strategize well ahead of time to maximize the solar gain during the microsummer periods. At best, it is a bit cumbersome and can mean a lot of work for someone just beginning to learn how to work with a variety of plants.

Winter is moderately good for larger plants to assume a vegetative growing period, because the sun is lower in the sky and penetrates deeply into the home. Although, with such short days, it is not optimal for real booming growth. Depending on planter size and style, winter can be a decent time to plant seedlings, but most ideal is to wait until you draw a bit closer to either the spring or fall equinox, when you will get maximum solar gain in the planter regardless of style. Having lived in a couple of different Package Earthships, I have found that, with expertise and a bit of luck, you can make these greenhouses quite productive, though they are more challenging and slow going.

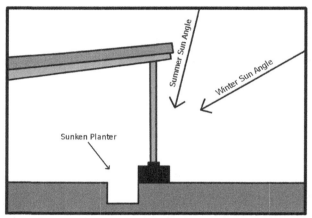

An elevation cut of a Package greenhouse with a sunken planter.

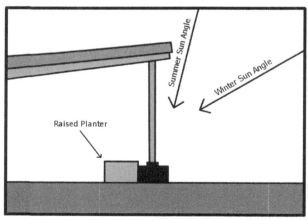

An elevation cut of a Package greenhouse with a raised planter.

As far as common planter orientation goes, there are a few more things to add to the discussion. If you plan to plant mainly perennial trees and shrubs, a sunken planter is a reasonable option (see drawing). The extra headroom a sunken planter provides allows for things like figs and dwarf bananas to expand a bit better than a planter with less headspace. The challenge lies in establishing smaller plants or cover crops to serve as a support in creating a healthy rhizosphere. To do that properly can be difficult due to the lack of sunlight. Timing the sowing of smaller plants so that you get the most biomass production possible when the microsummer periods come around is key. The raised planter is not optimal for someone serious about growing the absolute maximum yields. This style is more suited for a homeowner who may plant a few annuals, as time allows. Growth and ripening are generally slower due to the sunlight issues elaborated above. Therefore, if the grower has limited time to dedicate to the greenhouse, a mixture of low maintenance and easy-to-care-for plants, with a few annuals here and there, may be a great alternative to a highly managed greenhouse.

GLOBAL DOUBLE GREENHOUSE

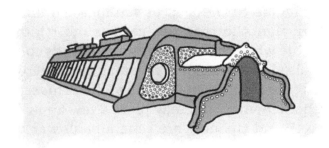

The Global model is the bread and butter of modern Earthship design. These buildings are the culmination of nearly forty years of fine-tuning and enhancements. Combined with the improvements that sustainable technologies have made in recent years, these advanced buildings are almost as seamless in distinction and comfort as on-grid homes— a massive leap forward in technology and performance.

These structures make use of two layers of south-facing glass. The exterior glass shares the same sloped installation as the Modular design, which creates the first primary greenhouse. Then there is a second layer of glass set back several feet behind the main greenhouse within the home. This second wall of glass is installed vertically with no slope, just like the Package design, and it further divides the interior space from the main greenhouse (see drawing). In effect, the primary greenhouse becomes a hallway that spans the length of the home, and the second greenhouse becomes included in, and is divvied up, between the actual living spaces.

Utilizing this design drastically reduces temperature fluctuations throughout the year, nearly doubles the active growing area, and creates multiple microclimates to diversify over-all yields. Although, in some cases, the design of the living space omits garden space from the interior of the home. Opting to re-duce the total garden planter space by excluding the planters behind the second layer of glass is a matter of personal prefer-ence, and may be suitable for people who want all the benefits of a double greenhouse, but do not want the extra room for plants in the living space.

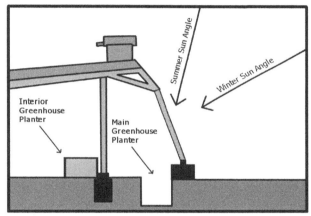

An elevation cut of a typical Global greenhouse.

As you can see in the drawing, the foremost greenhouse planter is just like the Modular greenhouse. But, with the add-ition of a second layer of glass, the solar gain is retained much better, and there is a significant reduction in temperature swings. The interior planter behaves very similarly to a Package Earthship greenhouse and comes active in the wintertime when the sun's angle is at its lowest. The end of fall and throughout winter is a great time to do a flush of greens, or, as you will see when we talk about different greywater setups, the interior planter can become an optimal candidate for a subsurface reed bed system—allowing for highly efficient greywater processing inside and dedicating the main greenhouse to maximum production. Overall, the Global model and its offshoots are excellent choices for someone serious about creating a robust, holistic greenhouse.

SIMPLE SURVIVAL AND CUSTOM GREENHOUSES

Many people are not skilled builders or do not have an infinite budget to dedicate to new construction. So, from this need/demand, the Simple Survival Greenhouse was created. This relatively new model went beyond meeting the needs of a group of people wanting a more accessible, more affordable Earthship. It has become the go-to for humanitarian builds and disaster relief. It works great from the standpoint that it makes the Earthship technologies translatable and accessible to people who are not wealthy and in areas that are not resource rich.

However, the Simple Survival model is not exclusively for those with a tight budget. Many people all around the world have taken these designs and made very high-end, beautiful homes. This greenhouse style is a part of probably the most iconic Earthship ever made—the Phoenix Earthship. The Phoenix has an epic rainforest feel inside, while the outside landscape is high desert, with nothing but sagebrush in sight. Many, many people have been blown away by the environment inside the Phoenix. Two cockatiels and a parakeet live full-time in the jungle-like setting, and a big fish pond hosts a turtle or two. Since this building is approximately 5,800 square feet, it is out of the average folks' budget. Nevertheless, it does present a remarkable example of the full potential of this style of greenhouse and of off-grid living in general.

Some newer models are built utilizing this greenhouse style, but do not contain all the other components that would classify them as a Simple Survival model. If you are planning on building in the future, you may want to find out what the modern models have to offer. If I had my choice of which style to build, live, and work in, I would, for sure, choose the Simple Survival Greenhouse.

The primary difference between this style and the Global model is in the exterior (main) greenhouse. The main greenhouse uses vertical glass and sloped glass. The sloped glass is part of the overhead kickup. Adding a glass kickup allows for the best light penetration into the home and planter. This greenhouse most closely approximates the daylight hours that plants get any time of year. It is the model that creates the most harmonious interplay with the natural pattern of plant growth. Also, as we saw in the Global model, with the addition of an extra layer of glass, you get all the added benefits of more growing space and temperature stabilization. The kickup provides extra headroom that can incorporate a more extensive array of plants that are not an option in other models.

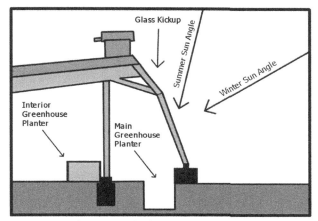

An elevation cut of a Simple Survival greenhouse.

One issue that can occur in all Earthship greenhouse designs (less likely in the Package model) is that if the greenhouse is left unventilated during hot summer days, temperatures can soar and plants suffer. Since there is more greenhouse glass in the Simple Survival model than the other models, it is prone to heat up faster and more intensely. In the microclimate section, we will look at options to help mitigate or alter any zones that are extreme in one way or another.

WALIPINI/UNDERGROUND GREENHOUSE

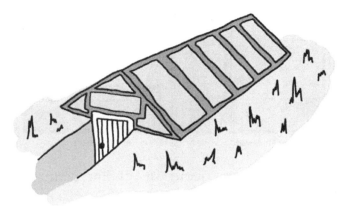

A Walipini is an underground greenhouse. Glass or plastic is installed overhead to enclose the excavated space and create a sunken effect. This style of construction comes in a whole host of shapes and sizes, making it a versatile and appealing option for those who are looking for the closest approximation to an Earthship. Walipinis, being underground, make use of the stable earth temperature, as in a cave. As solar gain penetrates the greenhouse, some of that heat gets stored in the walls and helps to balance the inside temperature perpetually. Using thermal mass and solar gain together reduces the demand for any auxiliary heating and cooling. If you are looking for an alternative to Earthships for interior garden cultivation, then a Walipini may be the best option for you.

LEAN TO GREENHOUSE

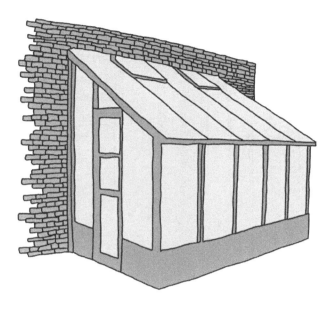

Another excellent option, if Earthships are not part of your design, is a Lean-to greenhouse. It offers nearly the same performance level as most of the Earthship greenhouse styles outlined here. The name describes the construction style. It is generally an addition to a home that leans towards and connects to an exterior south-facing wall. There are many adjustments to the dimensions and shape of a Lean-to greenhouse, depending on climate, cost considerations, and placement. However, the standard orientation is the same as the exterior Simple Survival greenhouse that has a vertical glass layer combined with a sloped glass kickup. In comparison with Earthship style greenhouses, a Lean-to will generally have a significantly reduced area of growing space. Nevertheless, the practices and techniques discussed in this book can certainly be applied, just on a smaller scale.

DETACHED GREENHOUSE

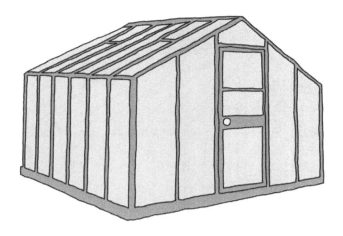

There are a variety of styles when it comes to Detached greenhouse structures. Things like geodesic domes, hoop-houses, high-polytunnels, and smaller kit greenhouses all fit under the umbrella of a Detached greenhouse. Their suitability is likely less than ideal, in comparison to the other styles for the type of greenhouse management outlined in this book. In general, a Detached greenhouse already comes with a specific purpose or goal. A small, hobby greenhouse is designed as a staging area to start seedlings and nurse plants; a more massive polytunnel greenhouse is usually used to grow a single crop at a time, rather than a mixture of perennials and annuals of all shapes and sizes. A high-end conservatory for cultivating rare and unique plants could include elements from this management style, but the focus of this book is on home-scale practices for the average gardener or homesteader.

Another factor that affects the overall suitability of this management style is the invested energy input required. A Detached greenhouse does not have passive heating and cooling through the thermal mass, as an Earthship or Lean-to style does.

So, auxiliary heating is necessary during colder periods, adding to the overall cost and upkeep.

Ultimately, the individual needs to discern if using a Detached greenhouse in a manner outlined in this book is worth the time and effort. It is possible, but numerous extra design adaptations would need incorporation to have success with a Detached greenhouse system.

GREENHOUSE STYLE
PERFORMANCE BREAKDOWN

The table below rates some fundamental performance values for each style of greenhouse. This breakdown is specifically for the greenhouse, not the entire home. It shows the general expectations for each style, given the standard of each model. It is designed to be a quick reference and a comparative summarization of this chapter. All Earthships and greenhouses are unique, and various input concerns could alter these ratings. Models can be hybridized. Also, any structure could be built from higher- or lower-quality materials, adjusting these general ratings. For example, what I rate as the highest performing and most expensive greenhouse style can be inexpensive to build. So, any style greenhouse could be used to replace the standard one associated with each model, if done so carefully. Again, all of this is my subjective opinion based on my personal experience with each type. You will need to be discerning as they may vary with climate, region, and personal preference.

Greenhouse Style Performance Breakdown

Performance Aspect → / Greenhouse Style ↓	Solar Gain Ultilization	Seasonal Planter Performance	Temperature Stabilization	Construction/ Installation Skill	Cost
Modular	Medium	Medium	Medium	Medium	Medium
Package	Very Low	Very Low	Medium	Low	Low
Global	High	High	Very High	Very High	Very High
Simple Survival	Very High	Very High	High	High	High
Walipini	High	Medium	High	Medium	Medium
Lean-To	Very High	Medium	Medium	Low	Low
Detached	Very High	Medium	Low	Low	Low

This chart rates each greenhouse on a scale from very low to very high over a set of fundamental critera. Review attached section for more details.

CHAPTER II

GREENHOUSE GREYWATER PLANTERS

The information on greywater and how to properly use it is often cloudy and conflicted from one source to another. I receive a high volume of questions about greywater regularly, and because people have many different reasons for incorporating a greywater system into their greenhouse or landscape, this chapter is intended to clarify the fundamentals, as well as pose effective options.

The general perception is that greywater systems are a form of good stewardship for managing wastewater. Some may want a greywater system inside the home to recycle water for use in toilets; others may wish to use the greywater for supplemental irrigation in the greenhouse or garden. Still others may choose to use a greywater system as a means of responsible disposal to protect and safeguard the local environment from pollutants. Perhaps the goals for the system are all three.

Integrated water harvesting and contained wastewater treatment are essential features in all Earthship designs. Processing greywater and blackwater within the home are core practices that have existed in Earthship construction consistently over the years. Throughout the thread of the Earthship's evolution, we see the development of planter cells and their role in managing greywater to refill and flush the toilet. This efficient and frugal interplay between sink/shower, planter and toilet is seen as one of an Earthship's most exceptional sustainability features. It will forever boggle my mind that it is taking so long for our civilization to come up with a better alternative than going to the bathroom in what is basically drinking water.

My stance on household greywater systems, from nearly a decade of working with traditional Earthship-style greywater planters and studying the wisdom of many experts on the topic, is that simple and straightforward exterior-fed (all greywater is processed outside the structure) greywater systems are the ideal setups. Sophisticated interior or exterior systems can and do work, but, in my opinion, the cost and complexity greatly outweigh the benefits.

There are scenarios that may legitimately force some people to install an internal greywater system instead of an exterior one, such as harsh or extreme environmental factors. An excessively long freezing temperature season or an ultra arid, desertified zone are examples. Both show inhospitable surroundings incapable of hosting vegetation successfully. If you are in a situation where a greywater greenhouse is appropriate, do not be deterred from coming up with a workable solution, as it may be the best option for the overall design of your home. Understanding greywater and how to use it is valuable knowledge, regardless of if you already have, plan to have, or not have a greywater system.

My preference for residential buildings is to install composting toilets, with a basic, easily serviceable greywater system that feeds outdoor plants. There are many different styles of composting toilets available on the market to suit the specific needs of the homeowner. Some require minimal interaction and upkeep, while others require more work and can create a valuable end product for your garden or landscape in the form of well-cured humus. For the majority of the general population, not having a flush toilet in the home is a major sticking point, and could be a deal-breaker for living a more ecologically minded lifestyle. If this is the case, an internal greywater system that feeds the toilets may be the best option or, possibly, an exterior-fed system with freshwater used to refill the toilets. In either scenario, take extra care to be sure that your water sources are sufficient to meet the demands of your usage.

Note: By no means is the inclusion of a greywater planter mandatory for operating a holistic greenhouse. The bulk of the material covered in this book functions independently from these greywater planter systems and applies to any residential greenhouse operation.

GREYWATER GUIDELINES

Greywater systems should not be designed to store greywater in isolation or intermingled with another substrate. How greywater enters and moves through the planters is very important, because stagnant greywater can and will go septic within twenty-four hours. An improperly designed greywater system could become a breeding ground for all kinds of pathogens and diseases, posing a severe health risk, especially indoors. Only a select few plants are innately capable of thriving in septic wastewater. So, if your greywater system becomes a blackwater system due to poor design, most of your plants will get stressed and sick.

Greywater should always enter the system subsurface and go directly into biologically active soil. Top watering with greywater presents a health risk to humans, and it can develop a foul smell, enticing unwanted and potentially harmful pests into the home. When greywater enters directly into active living soils, a whole host of bacteria, worms, insects, and fungi can get to work processing and absorbing it, making any nutrients in the greywater far more plant soluble than in raw or even pretreated greywater.

A critical aspect in the healthy functioning of any greywater system is the type of laundry and dish detergent and soaps used. When purchasing or making these products, be sure they are free of sodium ingredients. Over time, salt buildup can severely compromise your system. The more natural and plant-based the product is, in addition to being sodium-free, the better. Numerous companies specialize in these types of products. At your local health food store, there should be at least one option that meets the salt-free requirements of the greywater system.

Anyone new to greywater systems should also be made

aware of the very particular plumbing methods and materials required to achieve a smoothly running system. A lot of traditional plumbing knowledge translates into greywater installation, but some key aspects do not. Maintaining the correct amount of fall and slope of the pipes is important. Fitting types, piping types, and sizes are also essential. There are a series of fine details that can either optimize or frustrate the whole process. Even if you have a solid background in plumbing systems, it is well worth the effort to research greywater construction/installation and take the time to understand the differences between regular household plumbing and greywater plumbing before jumping into a project.

When installing a greywater system, the laws and regulations vary from region to region, so it is essential to check with your local municipality to ensure you are working and building under proper legal boundaries. For example, in the early days of greywater legislation in New Mexico, water from the kitchen sink was included for greywater use. This has been updated, so that kitchen sink drainage now goes straight to septic lines. If you were unaware of a change like this, it could cause some unwanted snags in your permitting, construction, or inspection process.

What follows in the remainder of this chapter are a few profiles of possible alternative greenhouse planter options. These may meet the goals, needs, or aspirations of those interested in incorporating a new greywater system in their home, or who have questions about one they already have. These sections will not provide construction drawings to build from, but rather present an overview of greywater principles, functionality, and possible options in design and layout. If you plan to explore one of these alternatives, it is advisable to consult with a wastewater/greywater professional to ensure the best outcome for the specifics of your build. Every situation has its own set of concerns, and it is up to you if you choose to incorporate a greywater system in your home.

TRADITIONAL EARTHSHIP PLANTER

The technical term for these planters is called evapotranspiration cells. The concept behind them is very similar to wicking beds. The idea is there is a pool of water beneath the soil and, by capillary action and temperature changes, the water will work its way up into the topsoil from below, and plant roots in search of hydration will push down through the soil and find the water underneath (See drawing).

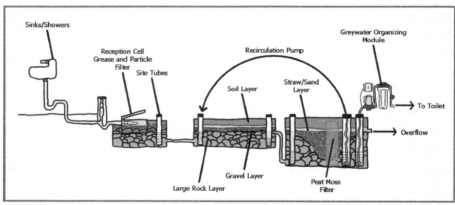

A profile view of an example evapotranspiration planter configuration.

Greywater from sinks and showers goes first to a reception cell, which acts as a grease and particle trap to keep the system from becoming clogged. It serves as a pretreatment area to clarify the usable from the unusable greywater for the rest of the system.

The greywater then makes its way through a rock layer, under the grease and particle trap, and overflows into the first evapotranspiration planter. This initial planter is typically shallow and labeled as the "Salad Bar" section. This planter and any further planters attached to this system are gravity fed, by creating a sloped grade at the bottom of each cell and progressively deepening the angle as the water flows towards the end. Each planter cell is rubber-lined to prevent the water from escaping into the ground or the house.

The layers of a lined planter are built up from the bottom —larger rocks, smaller rocks, straw, sand, and then soil. The exact ratios vary depending on the home and where the planter falls in the flow and order of the greywater system. The straw layer forms a barrier so that the sand and soil do not mix and become one big homogenized mass.

At the final and deepest cell is a peat moss filter for an added layer of cleanup and absorption of any particulates. Also at the end are two pumps—one is a small recirculation pump that pushes the greywater at set intervals back through the system to keep it from stagnating; the second pumps the water from the deepest cell to the greywater board, which pressurizes and further filters the greywater to then refill the toilet.

Intermittently, throughout the planter cells, site tubes are installed as access points and to gauge the water level. Properly formed layers can be charged with greywater so that, beneath the straw, all the greywater flows through and fills the spaces between the rocks at the bottom.

When working with this type of planter, it is crucial to know the sizing and spacing of each cell as well as the flow of water. Understanding the pattern and orientation of greywater in the planters becomes critical during the greenhouse design phase to select the correct plants for proper placement in the planter cell. Without this information, it is easy to make time-consuming and discouraging mistakes that can affect your total progress and the overall health of your system.

Although the traditional Earthship planter is the most expensive to install and requires the most upkeep, in comparison to the other styles presented in this section, it is a viable option for areas that have extremes in seasonal climatic conditions.

BOX TROUGH PLANTER

Although uncommonly found installed in an Earthship greenhouse, this greywater system design is an attractive and viable candidate. The concept behind this setup is simple and straightforward. A box trough is a long and narrow empty box, sunken within the soil, that spans the length of the planter. It has a removable lid for easy access, monitoring, and servicing the system. The underground void that the trough creates inhibits plant roots from colonizing the space and clogging the system, because they cannot travel over air. The household greywater lines get drained directly into the box subsurface and pour out onto a small splash plate to prevent erosion. The greywater then floods the trough and slowly seeps into the soil.

If your system lacks a pretreatment chamber (which may not be required, depending on your greywater laws), then periodically the trough will need to be mucked out, and the contents added to an exterior compost pile.

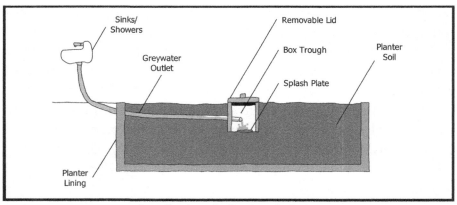

A profile view of a box trough planter.

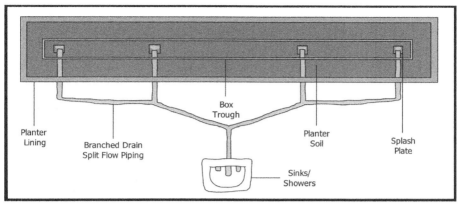

An overhead view of a box trough planter without the trough lid.

The most cost-effective type of box trough system is either one that individually pipes all the household greywater directly into the box trough, or combines the drains into a branched drain system. Some features that may need to be incorporated, depending on your build, are a reception cell for pretreatment, a dosing siphon, or a dipper box for proper surge capacity and flow regulation.

If you do not require greywater for reuse in the toilets, this system can be an excellent alternative to the traditional Earthship-style greywater planter. It is also a sound choice if the cost is a barrier, because it is significantly cheaper. Even if all the extra components were required to have this style system perform correctly, it would likely still come in well under the budget of a traditional Earthship greywater planter.

Daniel Dynan

INTERIOR MULCH BASIN
PLANTER

The mulch basin design, as with the box trough system, is unable to provide greywater to reuse in the toilet, but works optimally for responsible disposal as long as the correct plants are utilized to absorb the greywater.

This option is the most affordable, next to a low-tech basic exterior-fed design. The main feature that keeps costs down in a mulch basin planter is the ability to construct it as an in-ground planter, so there is no need to rubber-line, seal, or encase the planter bed unless the specifics of your site demand it. It also does not require a pretreatment cell, so the raw greywater can pour directly into the mulch. These two aspects significantly reduce cost, labor, and the potential for system failure. Although, depending on the volume and contents that go through your system, you may want to opt for adding an infiltration chamber at the greywater outlet tube to deter any interested pests from working their way into the home.

All systems, regardless of size and style, will require some degree of upkeep, and the frequency will vary. The mulch basin design calls for an annual replenishment of mulch and, potentially, some shoveling and re-mounding to maintain the correct dimensions.

This type of planter is laid out with a series of sunken rings in different locations. Elevated above each ring is a drainage outlet for the household greywater. The elevated outlets provide a similar effect as the empty space within the box trough, allowing the greywater to flow freely into the soil without any plant roots clogging the path. Make sure to place a small, flat rock or piece of wood in the basin ring where the water hits the mulch as a splash pad to buffer erosion. This type of planter is well-suited for a perennially dominated greenhouse an significantly reduces maintenance and upkeep times.

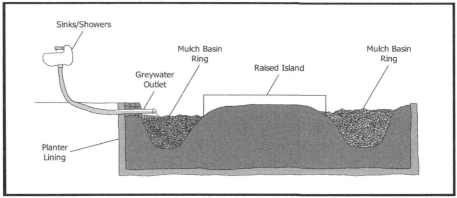

A profile view of a mulch basin planter.

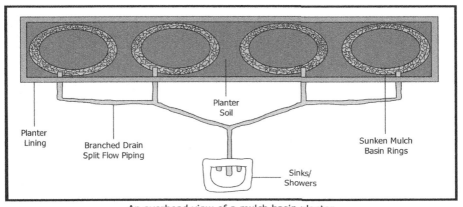

An overhead view of a mulch basin planter.

WETLAND BASED MODELS

The designs presented here have been tested and proven extensively for treating clarified septic effluent and make great options for processing greywater in a greenhouse. Both of these systems have been outlined many times over, in extreme detail, throughout a variety of publications. There is no inclusion of surface flow wetlands in this section, because they pose a serious health risk inside the home, even if it is greywater instead of blackwater.

For any system that intends to reuse greywater for flushing toilets, it is my recommendation to use a wetland planter in some form or to some degree. This is because, in nature, wetland ecosystems form at the bottom of watersheds where all the gunk, debris, and material that has been picked up along the way ends up. As such, these plants and the biome that forms in these zones are particularly suited to clean and process wastewater. Utilizing a wetland planter for greywater or blackwater treatment is an excellent form of biomimicry, because wetlands are one of nature's purification centers. If you want to clean water, why not do it the way nature does it?

When using wetland systems to treat greywater, note that greywater does not have the same concentration of nutrients as blackwater does. So, applying supplemental nutrition in some form may need to be part of your routine at appropriate intervals as part of the regular upkeep and support of the plant systems.

SUBSURFACE FLOW WETLAND

The image below depicts a sample layout. Note that every greywater system has its own set of concerns that need attention when designing and implementing it. In some cases, a separate, more robust pretreatment may be required for an operation that will receive heavier loads of grease or solids. For high-flow systems, a larger infiltration area may be needed to handle the maximum surge capacity.

Starting on the left side of the image, water that drains from sinks and showers goes directly into an infiltration galley that is in the planter itself. This has a removable lid for easy check-ups and clean-outs if needed. The planter bed is rubber-lined with a pond sealing material like EPDM, or sealed with plaster. The bottom slopes deeper towards one end. These cells remain relatively shallow, starting at a depth of one foot and going to a maximum of three feet deep on the far end. Over time, it has been shown that both greywater and blackwater effluent receive a higher level of treatment in shallower gravel beds. If the beds exceed the depth of three feet, the wetland species installed in the system will not be able to fully colonize the planter, reducing the overall uptime of the greywater with the most active areas of the microflora and root systems that provide the bulk of the cleaning.

Evenly spread, small washed gravel goes into the planter bed. Recommended gravel size is one-half to one inch. In a high-flow household, make larger infiltration areas at the inlet and outlet zones with a section of 1.5-to-3-inch gravel. Larger gravel at the inlets and outlets allows for the greywater to drain into the planter cell more quickly and smoothly. At the bottom of the end of the planter is an outlet tube that floods the wet well. The tubing inside the wet well regulates the height of the water in the cell. As the cleaned greywater fills up, it slowly overflows and drains towards its next destination. The wet well also has a removable access lid, which allows you to pull off the water regulation tubing and drain the system. This is done intermittently to flush out the greywater, as long as the bulk of the planter has sufficiently cleaned it. The flooding out of the planter cell helps to reset the system and allows the plants to establish their roots deeper in the cell.

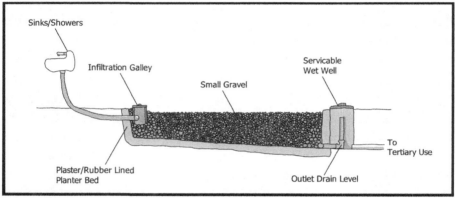

A profile view of a subsurface flow wetland planter.

Incorporating this type of planter into your greenhouse system has some advantages and disadvantages over the traditional Earthship model. The main benefits are its overall cost, more straightforward low-tech design, no-hassle plant systems, and high-quality, third-use output. One reason the total cost is less than other orientations is there is minimal usage of pumps, with the majority of systems needing none at all, due to the ability to gravity feed. There are fewer types of materials involved, which helps to keep costs down as well. The low-tech design is much less prone to failure, because there are fewer moving parts and dependence on consumptive mechanical components to operate effectively. The critical features, such as the infiltration gallery and wet well, can easily be manually operated and cleaned out as needed. Wetland plants are low-maintenance and pest-tolerant, making managing this type of planter straightforward.

The chief disadvantage of this style is the limitation of plant selection to only wetland, aquatic, and bog plants. With a smaller range of plants at your disposal, the diversity of yields and variety of species is diminished. So, it may not be an ideal option for a greenhouse manager looking to maximize food production. On the other hand, this model offers the best and most reliable means for recycling greywater for reuse in toilets.

If planning to process greywater within the home, consider a hybridized greenhouse planter system, which includes at least a small wetlands planter to clean greywater effectively. Interior wetlands are also a good option for a greenhouse manager who has a large-scale garden operation outside and could dedicate the interior space to processing the greywater from the home for supplemental irrigation of the garden during the growing season.

VERTICAL FLOW MIX MEDIA WETLAND

This style of greywater processing is technical and typically reliant on a pump to distribute the greywater to and throughout the planter. This inhibits me from recommending it to anyone, but it is in the greywater section because it is thoroughly proven and shown to be very useful. As far as I know, this style has not been installed in an Earthship yet, but does present an interesting concept for the right person. This type of bed may be the best option for someone with minimal space who wants a high degree of cleaning power for the greywater. It could also be a good option if the system could run entirely gravity-fed instead of using a pump, but I think that would be a rare scenario. Most likely, it would require some tweaking and the addition of a dipper box or dosing siphon, which still adds to the overall complexity and the possibility of system failure.

Essentially, a vertical flow bed uses various sizes of media in layers, from small and fine to big and coarse, with a top dosing delivery system for the greywater flow. The water gets distributed in the fine top layer of media and trickles down through the progressively larger layers. Hence, the "vertical" in its name —the water flows from the top to bottom of the bed. The different sizes and types of media offer a more complex habitat for biological organisms, which, in turn, compounds the cleaning and digestion process in a tiny space. Most of the time, for the inflow water to get spread evenly across the bed, a pump is used. The pretreatment area of the greywater system needs to be able to host that pump, which needs to be near a power source. These are all important considerations.

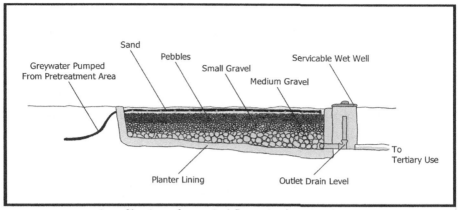

A profile view of a vertical flow mixed media planter.

The bed depth shares the same sizing as the subsurface flow bed, which is 1 to 3 feet deep, though starting around 2 feet is better to provide ample spacing of the aggregate layers. From top to bottom, the layers are comprised of mulch or sand about 3 inches deep, next 1/4-inch gravel for 6 inches, followed by 1-inch gravel for 4 inches, and, finally, 2-inch gravel for 6 inches. These figures and sizes will vary depending on who you talk to and what you have available locally, but if you plan to install a system like this, it is best to consult with a professional ahead of time. Of course, since this is in the wetland models subsection, this system is dependent upon the use of wetland, bog, or marsh plants for correct performance.

EARTHSHIP RETROFITTING

As briefly mentioned, there is potential to upgrade an existing Earthship greywater system to increase overall performance and longevity. When it comes to retrofitting, circumstances vary depending on the age, size, shape, and orientation of the system. Each situation requires special attention to detail to ensure success. Some people reading this chapter may already have lived in an Earthship and think all these planter designs are well and good, but how can an established planter cell that needs renovating get retrofitted without a massive overhaul?

Doing a complete overhaul of an older system and transforming it into one of the alternatives presented here is an excellent investment to make in your Earthship. In some cases, it will be labor intensive, costly, and likely very complicated, but that is not always the case. The wetland models provide the basis for making an affordable adaptation to the reception cell area that offers a great deal of health-engendering effects for an older greywater system, without exorbitant costs or extreme amounts of time and labor.

It is common, after a couple of years of use, for evapotranspiration-based greywater systems to have anaerobic pockets form in the gravel media layer of the beds. This layer is inaccessible unless you dig up the soil, making it tremendously challenging to service or replace the media. As time goes on, the progressive buildup of anaerobic activity eventually overwhelms the system and causes a decline in health and functioning. Activated charcoal, peat moss, and greywater filters depreciate in performance over time, and are also complicated or expensive to replace. The eventual clogging up of either a greywater or blackwater system is pretty much guaranteed, but how you orient the system and what techniques you use can make the difference between five years before a needed over-haul or thirty-five years.

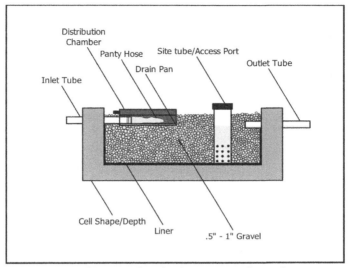

Distribution Chamber
Panty Hose
Site tube/Access Port
Drain Pan
Outlet Tube
Inlet Tube
Cell Shape/Depth
Liner
.5" - 1" Gravel

A profile view of wetland reception cell retrofit.

Since the reception cell is the starting point for the flow of greywater within the greenhouse, it is logical to make any retrofit focus on this area first and foremost. The particular retrofit depicted in the image is essentially a micro subsurface wetland planter and reception cell in one. The concept is simple—maximize the surface area and contact time the fresh grey-water has with the wetland plants before it enters any further into the system. The more time the greywater has in this modi-fied reception cell, the cleaner and more aerobic it becomes. Instead of flooding the evapotranspiration planters with pre-treated greywater that still has bacteria and other constituents that promote or accelerate anaerobic activity, the planter beds are flooded with at least partially cleaned and aerated water or, potentially, highly cleaned and aerated water. This little modi-fication goes a long way when it comes to the speed in which a greywater system will clog and become foul. The water that enters the media layer, after it has run through a wetland section, dramatically increases the health and performance of the whole system. With cleaner water entering the media layer, unhealthy levels of smelly bacterial mass have a harder time building. Any plants that do make contact with the water via their roots will be under less stress because the water is cleaner, and any additional pumps and filters added to the system will last significantly longer before failing.

GREYWATER HYBRIDIZATION

My position on complex and sophisticated greywater systems is at the beginning of this chapter. While they are not my recommendation, in some scenarios, a greenhouse designer may want to have the effects of multiple planter designs to fill a variety of needs. To best achieve a well-functioning greywater system that has several design goals, you could incorporate various planter styles with well-thought-out overflow systems, or split the household greywater flows to different types of greywater planters, depending on suitability.

Accomplishing this could quickly become costly and technical, but the results could, in turn, end up being a constructive use of resources. One example of a hybrid greenhouse greywater system could follow the lines of something like this: Someone installs a small subsurface reed bed to clean the sink greywater exclusively for reuse in the toilet, then directs the rest of the household greywater to a larger planter set up as one of the other styles outlined above. Another example could be partitioning the entire planter space into a combination of a wetland planter that purifies the greywater first, and then the overflow spills into a mulch basin planter for responsible disposal. There are many different configuration possibilities for you to consider as you design your greywater system.

CHAPTER III

GREENHOUSE DESIGN STRATEGIES

Design strategies for a holistic greenhouse are comprised of four predominant elements—plant archetypes/guilds, microclimates, zones of use, and maximizing grow space. Mastering and incorporating these into your management style will aid you in generating as much resilience, beneficial interactions, and yields as possible. Learning these design skills takes time and patience and a continual effort on the part of the greenhouse manager.

Many may opt to install all low-maintenance, ornamental, and pest-tolerant plants to reduce time and energy, because of their busy schedules. Others will take pride and joy in a lush and vibrant greenhouse stacked full of unique and productive plants. As covered in the introduction, the intention of the management styles presented here is to be as holistic and ecologically sound as possible, while exerting a moderate to high amount of attention to the greenhouse development. The complete protocol presented may not suit everyone, but I believe anyone will be able to find some useful, practical tools throughout this work, regardless of the level of interaction you choose in your greenhouse.

PLANT ARCHETYPES
AND FUNCTIONS

There are many things to consider when selecting plants for indoor cultivation. Understanding a plant's temperament, mature growth size, light and nutrition requirements, and so on are foundational to successful incorporation into the greenhouse. Researching a variety of candidates beforehand and assessing their suitability is a wise thing to do. The subsequent sections will build upon the information here, and you will see how each aspect will interplay with the next, creating a dynamic and well-organized greenhouse.

Below, we have plant profile examples. These are divided into seven archetypal groups, which translate into the basis for building guilds and plant layers in the greenhouse. The archetypes are primary resource consumers, bushes/shrubs, pest indicators, low maintenance/hardy, groundcovers, vining, and unique/novelty. The profiles highlight the strengths and weaknesses of each plant, based on the constraints of the greenhouse. Some plants are capable of fulfilling numerous functions, which make them highly desirable. When designing your plant system, be aware of which functions plants can provide and how well they will synergize with other plants.

Primary Resource Consumers

These plants generally become the focal point in the planter because of their multifaceted functionality and attractiveness. They demand the most water and nutrients, but generally provide the highest yields. Examples are bananas and figs.

Banana - *Musa* sp.

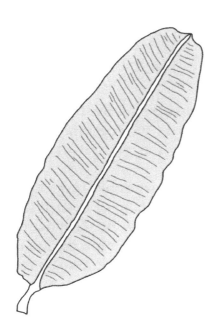

Bananas in Earthships are iconic, and I think they contribute to the fame and appeal of these homes. Each climate may alter the suitability of installing bananas to some extent, but by and large, for the northern hemisphere, bananas are an ideal option.

When selecting a banana variety, note mature height. The planter depth can help to restrict larger types if you do choose one, but very tall species will likely become cramped and be less productive. There are many dwarf options available in nursery catalogs, and I would recommend starting with one of those. All of the bananas seen in the Earthships of New Mexico stem from one original plant, many years ago, and have been propagated over and over again by removing a baby banana plant emerging from the mother plant rhizome. The variety grown at Earthship Biotecture is a dwarf cavendish. It has been climatized and adapted to the high altitude with drier than average interior conditions.

The greenhouse manager can slowly fine-tune and condition the successive generations of the plants grown to adapt to the specific area and greenhouse. This works with plants propagated vegetatively or through seed production, and is a great tactic to increase the overall resilience and productivity within the greenhouse space over time, but it does require consistency and dedication.

In the greenhouse setting, bananas can play an active central role because they provide a variety of functions. They produce lots of nutrient-rich biomass, which is excellent for compost and for recycling back into the soil. Bananas are easy to manage effectively for either primary greywater consumption or fruit production. They are highly consumptive of greywater and like well-saturated soil conditions.

It is ideal to have at least three bananas per root system —a large, medium, and small. Having one banana in each stage allows for the most productive fruiting rotation. Each banana tree will produce a single inflorescence once it is mature, and by that time several other banana plants will have grown up from the same root system. Chop the oldest banana down, once its fruits are ripe and harvested, allowing the mid-size one to reach maturity. Then, it becomes a cycle of fruiting and chopping as needed. From my experience, once the bananas have become accustomed to their climate, they are very low maintenance. They may occasionally suffer from a bout of a scale family pest, but recover quickly, and they only need some light pruning of leaves that die off from time to time.

When installing a banana within the greenhouse, it is essential to take note of its placement. In nature, bananas are an understory species, not a canopy species. Therefore, they prefer shadier conditions over full sun. I have seen many bananas suffer from sun damage because they were planted in a place with too much sun for their needs. The plant will become too stressed out to fruit, and its regular growth pattern will suffer. In the microclimate alteration section, there are some tools to deal with this if you are forced to place plants in suboptimal areas.

Fig - *Ficus carica*

Figs are another highly useful and productive plant for the greenhouse. There are many varieties available, each adapted to particular conditions, so it is crucial to select one suited to your circumstances. For the most part, figs do well in full sun, so they are a suitable choice as a central feature where bananas are not. Figs make a substantial and vigorous root system that can absorb lots of water, and their salt tolerance is higher than average, making them an ideal candidate for planters that incorporate greywater systems and have high flow inputs. The different strains of figs are also quite dynamic in that, in addition to having the ability to absorb and tolerate high water conditions, some are also able to tolerate dry conditions.

As with most plants, the depth and size of the planter can contribute to the manipulation of the fig's mature height and width. They can also handle heavy pruning, so you can control their maximum size that way as well. With pruning, you can thin the density of the canopy structure, allowing for optimal solar gain deeper into the home, while not com-

promising the productivity of the figs themselves. It is advisable, when planting figs in conjunction with other plants (as we will cover in the guild and plant layering section), to first establish all the other plants, giving them time to expand their root systems to a comfortable spacing before introducing the fig. Fig roots are aggressive and will squelch and restrict less robust plants.

Another factor to consider is that figs can emit a volatile essential compound that smells very much like cat urine. When I use figs, I use them sparingly and try to keep them positioned in an area where any emission will not disrupt activities taking place in that area of the living space.

Bushes/Shrubs

Under this archetype, you will find a plethora of species to choose from. The reason for the massive selection is the mature size of the plants and the ability to keep them trained via pruning. Most plants that fall in the bush or shrub category will fit ideally, size-wise, into the greenhouse, but may have some special requirements or features that preclude them from being the best candidates for your operation. For example, the need for specific soil conditions that do not mesh well with your other plants, spines, thorns, or any other hazardous part, as well as potential excessive growth habits.

Taking time to research thoroughly beforehand may seem like a chore, but you may find a surprise or two when you dig deeper into possible plants for this layer of the greenhouse. Bushes/shrubs can stack many functions, like providing berries, tea, medicine, pest defense, or nutrient-rich mulch for your system. Since there is a vast array of plants in this category, discovering some species that you find interesting and useful can be an exciting process during the design phase. Examples are lemon verbena and rosemary.

Lemon Verbena - *Aloysia citrodora*

These little shrubs often look thin and spindly, but are surprisingly sturdy. They can get quite large and robust under

certain conditions, but within the greenhouse setting it is unlikely unless they are cultivated and trained to do so. They generally average around four feet high, and two to three feet wide. The stalks are woody, and the leaves have an almost gritty rough texture. The leaves are used to make medicine and can be plucked right off the plant to make tea. The strong lemon flavor has been used in many culinary dishes through the years.

Lemon verbena's relatively small and unimposing footprint works well to give more demanding plants room to spread out. It has a slender, open branching structure, and with consistent harvesting, these plants can provide more light to stimulate growth on the ground cover layer. Ultimately, this feature aids in better water retention, more biodiversity in your greenhouse, and improved soil conditions via ground covers being able to grow more efficiently as living mulches.

Rosemary - *Rosmarinus officinalis*

Rosemary is a widely used, well-known herb. These plants have a dense, bushy nature and will provide plenty of herb for your culinary needs. Easy to manage, not very resource demanding, drought tolerant, and pest tolerant/repellant, they make a superb choice for a variety of microclimates within the greenhouse. An average size to expect when grown in the planter is about three to four feet wide by four feet tall. As rosemary can be raised to take up a smaller footprint, or allowed to expand and get quite large, it makes an excellent option for container planting. It can be nestled in an empty spot in the greenhouse as needed.

A potential downside is that they take over the planter area they grow in, in such a way that it is very difficult to include anything below them. So, rosemary acts as both a shrub layer plant and a ground cover. It may be one of the best options for someone looking to spend minimal time working in the greenhouse and still obtain a consistently useful yield.

Pest Indicators

In the greenhouse, the regular checks and balances of the outside world get modified or removed and can quickly create an optimal environment for various pest species. Often, the predator species or weather conditions that would regulate the pests naturally are nonexistent. The lack of natural balancing forces can make the pests all the more opportunistic. Even if other plants are healthy, they may try to spread their populations all around.

Pest Indicator plants can show the greenhouse manager the overall health level of the system as well as provide a lot of valuable data, if you carefully observe them. A flailing pest indicator could clue you into when to pre-emptively apply some nutrition to bolster the immune system of the greenhouse, which could help to address any emerging deficiencies. Through the early detection of pests on the plant, you could staunch potentially problematic pest explosions by eradicating the pest indicator plant. If there is an isolated outbreak on the pest indicator, and it does not spread to the localized area, you can glean that your soil community is maturing well and you have nothing to fear in terms of a greenhouse-wide pest invasion. On the other hand, if the pests start to migrate rapidly to other plants, there is a more profound imbalance in your system.

The following two examples are from my personal experience in a greenhouse I managed with this holistic style. These may or may not apply to your greenhouse specifically, because the establishment of different biological soil communities will cause individual plants to thrive and others to be stressed out. To further complicate it, the soil communities will most likely change over time as well. So a pest indicator that worked early on in a management paradigm may not work later, due to the changes taking place in your soil as it matures. In your greenhouse, though, you will inevitably come across a few plants you can utilize in this way. Once you have discovered some plants that showcase this feature, you would use them only in moderation in order to not invite excessive pest pressure into the greenhouse.

If you are unsure where to find a plant that could fill this role, an excellent starting place is a ruderal species, like a dandelion. Ruderal plants are the first to colonize disturbed land, initiating the soil rebuilding process and paving the way for more stable plant communities. These plants do well in poor soils, so as the soil in the planter gets healthy and more diverse, these plants get stressed out and attract pests. There are tons of ruderal plants all over the world, and you could even go out to a spot that has damaged or disturbed soil in your area, dig up a couple of plants, transplant them into your greenhouse, and see how they do. The two we will examine are winged tobacco and marigold.

Winged Tobacco - *Nicotiana alata*

Winged tobacco is similar to Nicotiana tabacum, which is what the typical cigarette is. This variety is very rarely cured and smoked though. It is predominantly an ornamental plant enjoyed because of its fragrant flowers. These are found commonly in gardens and, as I  stated in the introduction to this section, each greenhouse manager will need to figure out the particular plants that can fill the pest indicator role for a specific greenhouse. In several that I managed, this plant would germinate, grow very fast, and look healthy. Sometimes it would stay looking fit for a while, but the majority of the time, after its main growth spurt, it would start to look stressed. Then, before long, there was a cluster of ten or fifteen aphids all over the flowers, or suddenly a pack of whiteflies appeared under one of the big leaves.

 Before I realized this plant fulfilled the pest indicator function, I didn't think much of it and maybe only exerted a minimal amount of balancing measures. But, that led to those aphids or whiteflies spreading to all the plants in the area. What could have been a non-existent challenge became something I would wrestle with for a whole season or more. When I began to use this plant more constructively, as soon as a significant pest buildup appeared, I would chop the plant down, compost it, and start a health-bolstering protocol for the garden. By the time I would cut down the plant, it had usually grown to about five feet five

inches tall, and produced large amounts of biomass containing many minerals and nutrients that benefitted both the composting process and the quality of the end product.

Marigold - *Tagetes erecta*

Using a marigold plant inside the greenhouse was always interesting to me, primarily because its functionality changed from outdoors to indoors. Outdoors, the marigold can be seen as an insectary plant, bringing in all kinds of beneficial predators and pollinating insects. They have also been used in companion planting to assist in the growth and support of annual plants, like tomatoes, by deterring pests. I have found the opposite is the case when integrated indoors. As stated previously, the greenhouse creates a barrier from the natural flow of a whole host of inputs from nature. The pests that have subtly infiltrated and taken up residence within the greenhouse get an improved environment in which to thrive, without all the usual checks and balances from the outside.

Marigolds in the greenhouse often become a prime target of whatever pests may be rising to dominance and, as such, allow you to respond before the situation gets out of control. Marigold planted directly in the planter soil will more than likely end up being far more disruptive than it is worth, because you will soon have to dig it up, which will disturb the ground and leave a void. The strategy I recommend, when using marigold as a pest indicator species, is to plant it in a small pot near a set of plants or a particular area of the greenhouse, so that once you have identified a potential pest explosion, it can go back outside before too much damage is done. In the pest and disease section, we will look at more specifics surrounding the particular pests and issues that may arise, as well as how to handle them.

When you go to purchase a living plant (and to a lesser degree, a packet of marigold seeds), be aware of the difference between African marigold and pot marigold. African marigold is the common name associated with *Tagetes erecta*, even though the origins of the plant are in Central American. Pot marigold is the common name for *Calendula officinalis* and is not the species in this section. Pay careful attention when you are purchasing a marigold to ensure you are buying the correct plant, as they are vastly different in their performance and function within the greenhouse.

Low-Maintenance/Hardy

Low-maintenance/hardy plants are elements in your greenhouse garden that persist for long periods and require little attention. They are best used to stack a second or third function, possibly medicinal or nutritional. These types of plants are great staples to help reduce the overall time and energy needed in the greenhouse, because they don't require much work and help bolster the health of other plants. Two examples are tree philodendron and aloe.

Tree Philodendron - *Philodendron bipinnatifidum*

Philodendrons are part of a huge genus of plants, including elephant ears and many common houseplants. Widely available, these plants are affordable and work well to fill the low-maintenance/hardy niche, as most common houseplants will.

For those looking to fine-tune and make use of every square foot of grow space, tree philodendrons offer a creative species to build and design around. I spotlight this plant because of its unique morphology, which provides the chance to stack more functions in your greenhouse design.

These plants have sizeable, lobed fan-like leaves with long thin stems that connect to a base that protrudes above the soil. The leaves spread out in all directions, creating a big open area between the leaves and the bottom. Tree philodendrons work great for creating microclimates within the greenhouse and maximizing grow space. The big void between the leaves and stalk and the small root footprint in the planter allow for incorporating all kinds of other plants. You can add in a ground cover to maximize soil coverage or some tuber plants, like sweet potato vine, or even something like papaya, given proper planning.

Potentially, all the examples just mentioned could be combined into a little guild (more on guilds covered later in this chapter) with a small dense footprint. Often, the sheltered space under the tree philodendron's leaves is the perfect spot to nurse fresh cuttings or newly transplanted plants in pots. Tree philodendrons allow you to squeeze out the most from your planter, while maintaining healthy, diverse, and strong plants.

Aloe - *Aloe vera*

Aloe vera is more than just low maintenance and hardy. Most people will already be familiar with this plant for its use in skin care. Aloes can grow up to a few feet tall and wide, making them ideal for incorporating into the planter as a shrub layer plant. They are succulent and produce incredibly beautiful spike inflorescences. They are easy to propagate and manage by merely removing the smaller baby aloes that form from the mother rhizome. The gel-like substance inside the leaves aids in sunburn, and the juice is purchasable at health food stores as a beverage. They do well with little watering, thrive in full sun, and are pest tolerant. For these reasons, they make great additions in full-sun guilds because they help the surrounding plants by reducing overall inputs of resources, time, and pests.

Groundcovers

Groundcovers have a wide array of uses. They act as a living mulch to shield the soil from direct sunrays, which is extra important in the greenhouse because the sunlight is intensified by the glass and can lead to damage to the topsoil and the biological forces living there. If the greenhouse glass is of lower quality, this is especially the case. Sometimes small bubbles form in the manufacturing of glass panes, which can act as a lens magnifying sunlight intensity and severely burn the plants. Groundcovers can also help fungi pipe and exchange nutrients around in the rhizosphere. They ofte provide an extra yield in the form of tea or fruit as well. There are even some that are excellent at filtering airborne pollutants and improving air quality. The two we will examine are mint and purple queen.

Mint - *Mentha* sp.

There are many varieties of mint that can make suitable additions in the greenhouse space. Your choice depends on personal preference and availability. Plants like basil and tulsi are part of the broader mint family, but under a different genus and display a more erect shrub-forming nature. Examples of mints that can fulfill the ground cover role are spearmint, peppermint, pennyroyal, and wild mints. Most species in the Mentha genus are voraciously spreading ground covers in the greenhouse. Mints produce an abundance of leaves that are available to harvest regularly. The leaves can be dried and used in homemade teas or in fresh soups or mojitos. Timing is essential when deciding to plant a mint, because they are quick to grow, hardy, and spread aggressively. Therefore, it is best to allow the other plants time to establish themselves before introducing a mint, which could choke their growth patterns. Another ideal option for utilizing mint in the greenhouse space is in a hanging planter which can contain its spreading nature while obtaining a moderate yield.

Purple Queen - *Tradescantia pallida*

Purple queen is in the spiderwort family, popular in ornamental gardens as a ground cover. These plants are shade-tolerant, making them useful for filling nooks of the green-house otherwise unusable, and for incorporation with guild systems that have dense leaf spacing that absorbs and blocks sunlight from reaching the lower parts of the planter. Purple queen is highly effective as a biofilter for volatile organic compounds and, as such, is a valuable asset in an Earthship greenhouse for improving air quality. In working with these plants, I have never had a pest issue, and they thrive in a wide range of soil conditions. Purple queen is very dynamic and easy to work with, making it a useful addition to any greenhouse system.

Vining

Vining plants play into maximizing grow space and can also be a valuable asset for microclimate alteration. We will discuss both later. Yields can be produced both above ground and in the soil. An example of a plant that can provide an in-ground yield is a sweet potato vine that makes edible tubers. The two plants profiled here, passionflower and grapes, both produce fruits from vine. As well as vining, these plants can aid significantly in creating a pleasant atmosphere, filling spaces unusable by other plants.

Passion Flower - *Passiflora caerulea*

Over the years, I have not had much success with producing a lot of fruit from passion flower vines, but just the outstanding beauty of the flowers is enough for me to keep them alive and well in the greenhouse. There are many species, of all shapes and colors, available through nursery catalogs or websites. The most common is the blue passion flower. They are sturdy vines that can be woven in well with other plants. One, in a greenhouse I worked in, created such a dense mat of foliage over an entire eight-foot-by-ten-foot window area, it acted as a natural shade cloth, creating a lovely cooler microclimate in the planter zone beneath. When working during the day, I would often take quick breaks as I passed by that area to cool down a little bit. So, it works well for modifying excessively sunny regions of the greenhouse, but bear in mind that some of the leaves may receive sun damage as a result. This usually does not inhibit the vigor and overall health of the plant much, but it is something to monitor. Given ideal conditions, these vines can produce small fruits which make an excellent addition to smoothies or snacks.

Grapes - *Vitis vinifera*

Grapes are, of course, a classic addition in the greenhouse as a vining plant. Wine grapes, in general, have an incredibly

long history as an ethnobotanical species, and a big part of that history are the many styles of pruning, trellising, and training to maximize fruit production. Most of the grapes in Earthships are not pruned extensively to promote a central focus of fruit production, but they certainly could be. Grape vines, in this style of greenhouse management, fill more of a maximizing-grow-space role, and help in merging guilds of plants to weave the greenhouse space into a cohesive whole. Even with minimal pruning, the vines produce the occasional bunch of grapes, which is a nice bonus. All the grape leaves are edible, and the younger, newer leaves are the most palatable, especially for dolmas, a Mediterranean dish.

It is good to be aware that grape vines can act as ideal highways for the expansion of scale pests in the greenhouse. So it is crucial to check regularly for any signs of scale working its way on the grape and keep it under control.

Unique/Novelty

I added this section because a big part of greenhouse management is to have fun and enjoy what you are doing. These plants are exciting, rewarding, and fun to grow. A lot of people will be blown away at what is possible in a greenhouse setting. Although these plants generally are not high yielding and require a bit more attention, they are worthy of mention. The plants profiled here are pineapple and papaya.

Pineapple - *Ananas comosus*

Pineapples make for a conversation piece in the greenhouse because they have a similar wow factor as a big fruiting banana in the high desert. Pineapples fit in the shrub layer and have a small footprint. They are about the same as an aloe plant, maybe two feet by two feet. These have done quite well in the greenhouse and have frequently found a slot in the layout of newer ones.

The main downside is the long fruiting period and low yield. Each plant produces only one pineapple, which can take upwards of twenty-four months or longer until harvest, depending on temperature. Once you finally harvest the pineapple, save the top because you can start a new plant from it by rooting it in water and then plant it out again! Pineapples are pest-tolerant and require minimal attention in the greenhouse. If you don't mind the wait, it is always fun and rewarding to eat a pineapple you grew yourself. Plus, you can wow your friends by cultivating such an exotic fruit!

Papaya - *Carica papaya*

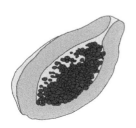

Papayas are tall, thin tropical fruit trees. Depending on your climate, these plants may struggle in the greenhouse. Out in the high desert of Taos, it was a mission to get these plants to fruit, but with some dedication, it did happen. As with any plant grown outside of its natural growing conditions, with that first big success of fruit or seed comes the promise of healthier, stronger plants in the future. The more that successive generations can be harvested and germinated, the more adapted the plants become to the environment.

Height is a consideration when growing papayas in the greenhouse, so they work well with planters that can restrict their size. They show a lot of promise in being able to compress many plants together in a small space horizontally, because of their thin vertical profile. If you think papayas may be a viable candidate for your greenhouse, know that they will require time and devotion to reach their full potential.

PLANT LAYERING AND GUILDS

In the previous section, we identified individual plant attributes and how they perform in the greenhouse setting. The next step is to see how all the plants interact and how they can support each other in creating a healthy synergy as a kind of team or guild. The goal of plant layering is to group the plants in the most optimal serviceable way for one another, thus improving overall conditions and performance as a unit. This is a starting point for looking at what you grow and how you grow it.

Plant layering is a form of biomimicry—the deliberate emulation of the patterns and ways of nature in design. In life, we see the formation of integrated communities that sustain and balance themselves in the environment. These plant guilds can be creatively designed to amplify strengths, reduce shortcomings, and overcome obstacles within the greenhouse system.

Guild Examples

This is an example of a composition for a full-sun guild. This setup would do well in a hot and very sunny area of the planter, while not compromising too much of the sunlight from flooding deeper into the home. The primary resource consumer and the most significant central element is a fig. It is essential that the fig is placed where it will get ample direct sun rays to ensure proper fruiting. An aloe and a lemon verbena could be planted to fill the shrub layer out at either side of the fig, allowing enough room for each plant to mature without being too cramped. A passion flower could be used as a vining plant and trellised along the wood framing of the window panes and, then, either across the glass or in whatever direction suitable for overall growth in the rest of the space. Mint as the ground-cover provides some competition in the rhizosphere for the robust roots of the fig, helping to keep each plant in check. The order and time of planting is important with this guild, because both the fig and mint can be overpowering in the rhizosphere. Once the other plants have a sound footing and have reached an appropriate size, the fig and mint can be incorporated.

A sample full sun guild comprised of a fig in the center, mint as the ground cover, aloe on the right, lemon verbena on the left, a passion flower vine, and two hanging planters above the shrub layer.

This grouping could be the core of the guild with the seasonal rotation of other shorter-life-cycle plants. For example, during peak growing season, a trellised tomato plant could be added and removed once it has finished fruiting. A seasonal rotational plant for optional use could be winged tobacco, towards the start of winter, to help get a heads-up on any pest populations looking to make some big power moves while the house is closed up and warm during the cold season.

The second composition is optimal for shady zones in the planter. A possible guild for this type of zone could look something like this: a banana for the primary resource consumer role and a great centerpiece because, in nature, it thrives in moderate sun to shade. Then, a tree philodendron on one side of the banana and rosemary on the other, again providing ample space so no plant is stunted or too crowded once it reaches mature size. So, we would have two shrub layer plants that can do well with less sunlight. The rosemary is providing a steady stream of leaves for culinary purposes, while being very easy to work with and happily warding off pests. The tree philodendron is pest-tolerant and creates a cozy microclimate beneath its leaves for groundcovers to spread all around and up to the rosemary. The groundcover could be purple queen, which would have no trouble colonizing the low-light topsoil zone while vastly improving air quality. A grapevine could be added and trellised around to weave in and out of shadier and sunnier areas, so that it could start to bridge the various zones of the planter into a cohesive unit. The plants in this guild could be all planted out at the same time, taking into account their full mature size, because none of these are extraordinarily competitive for space, either below or above ground.

A sample shady guild comprised of banana in the center, purple queen as the ground cover, rosemary on the right, tree philodendron on the left, a mushroom log, a grapevine and two hanging planters above the shrubs.

These plants would constitute the core of the guild and a

variety of plants could be introduced at ideal intervals to utilize all the space entirely. For instance, squash or pumpkin could
be planted out during a time of year when the shady zone would
get a little extra light and allow them to work their way out of
that zone to find the light. Once the plant has finished producing, compost the leftover organic material. A marigold in a pot
could be a great option to put near this guild at times you suspect increased insect activity, to gain a head start on what you
may be dealing with in the coming months pest-wise.

GREENHOUSE MICROCLIMATES AND ZONES

Earthships and greenhouses are found in diverse locations all over the world and come in all shapes, styles, and sizes. There is no one-size-fits-all program for where, when, and what to plant for every structure. The best option is to equip the greenhouse manager with a practical and straightforward method of observation and data gathering to make sound decisions for planting and designing, based on the specifics of any greenhouse. These techniques are a staple in the process of permaculture design. For a holistically oriented greenhouse, there are a few subtle, but key, differentiations to keep in mind. Learning to identify microclimates and zones can significantly increase the efficiency and performance of the greenhouse while avoiding some potential time-consuming and discouraging pitfalls.

Microclimate Identification

The method for microclimate identification involves categorizing all the active growing space of the planter into smaller climatic-based areas. This classification process encompasses overall temperature throughout the day, the total amount of direct sunlight, light penetration throughout the year, soil moisture level, the general feeling of the space, and any other descriptors that can characterize that area. The more, the better. In the image, there are eight highlighted areas—each labeled with some predominant characteristics. When you go to identify the microclimates in your space, label all the different areas as well as you can. There is no fixed limit you can label, so organize the space as you experience it. Also, it is best to come up with as many relevant adjectives for each micro-climate as possible.

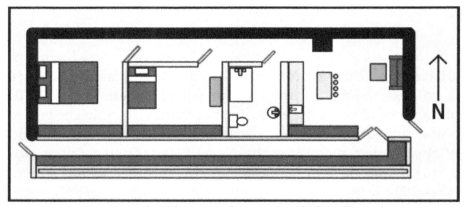

A common double greenhouse Earthship floorplan.

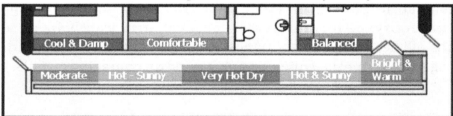

A double greenhouse layout labeled with microclimates.

The importance of this process comes to light when you superimpose plants or plant guild needs onto the designated microclimates. Then, you can see that a specific guild setup will inherently align to a particular section of the planter. If you think back to the plant guild section, if the two guilds described were in alternate positions—so that the shady-plant guild was in a full sun area and the full-sun guild was in a shady area—the performance would be disappointing. The main downside would be that the figs would not get enough sun to fruit and the bananas would get damaged by the sun, and, for both, growth would be subpar. Some of the other plants might get along okay, but optimizing their location and combinations takes the greenhouse from lackluster to abundant and robust.

Solar Aspect

During the microclimate analysis phase, whether you are building a new space or already have one to analyze, be sure to take the time to look up your local solar aspect. There are numerous resources available online and even some excellent smartphone apps that can assist (a link to these is in the Helpful Links section). Your solar aspect will show you the path of the sun and its location on any day at any time of the year, as well as total daylight hours for each day. This information can be valuable in organizing and setting expectations for specific areas within the greenhouse. Taking into account how the sun will move through it throughout the year will help you anticipate the likely microclimates that will form, and you can make sound decisions accordingly. If you are very familiar with the growing space and have never identified your microclimates, you will have data from the entire year to reflect on, as well as your current experience of the space. Not only will knowing your solar aspect help inform microclimates, if you plan to install a greywater system, it can aid in designing the layout and flow of the greywater through the greenhouse to ensure optimal performance.

Microclimate Alteration

Acknowledging that greenhouses, especially ones like diverse Earthship greenhouses, are not static places, but in a state of constant flux, helps the greenhouse manager understand better that microclimates will inevitably change over time, with or without the intervention of the gardener. The main takeaway is to think ahead and envision the direction the greenhouse is heading, while being flexible and adaptable to unforeseen developments, whether they are boons or detriments to the garden.

The most basic example of microclimate alteration is simply the use of shade cloth over a window that creates a particularly hot and sunny zone. Readily available materials found at your local shop are part of your toolkit, when approaching greenhouse design or dealing with potential issues. An alternative to purchasing shade cloth, touched on in the passion flower section, is to use a plant—generally a vining plant—to accomplish the same end. Many plants could fill that need and passion flower is just one them. There may be some sun damage to the plants in this scenario, but if chosen well,their overall health and vigor often remain high. Some easy pruning maintenance of leaves damaged more than fifty percent is all that needs to be kept up with occasionally. In many cases, this shade cloth effect of plants happens organically, without much planning, which leads to the next aspect.

The greenhouse microclimate does not stay static for long. Some developments can be anticipated—like an interior planter becoming shaded by the growth of plants in front of it. Other things will be complete surprises—like a tomato plant germinating from some compost you spread in a dark area of the planter, only to grow so massive it stretches through the interior hopper window to crawl across the ceiling of the exterior greenhouse, then proceed to totally cover an entire windowpane and produce prolific amounts of delicious tomatoes. With a little forethought, observation, and planning, the first example is made a non-issue by planting out a guild that, even at mature size, will still allow sufficient light to pass through to sustain the interior planter. Another option is knowing that the interior planter will likely become shaded after a few years of growing and plan to make that area a shade/mushroom garden.

The example of the giant tomato is a happy surprise, but there are certainly less than pleasant events that can come up as well. Having the right attitude and philosophy towards these changes can transform them into advantages instead of sources of frustration. Having a love for all things permaculture, I would be remiss in not tethering the message of this section to the permaculture principle of "the problem is the solution." This principle encapsulates a beautiful mindset that extends way beyond holistic greenhouse management, and can be an empowering and transformative outlook when applied to nearly every facet of life.

Greenhouse Zones

Zone identification is another valuable tool of the permaculture design process. It is worth the time for anyone serious about optimizing their greenhouse to consider zones and frequency of use. Essentially, the greenhouse manager would catalog the different sections of the greenhouse, based on how often they are visited and for what purpose. Each greenhouse is unique, and this is primarily dependent upon the style of Earthship or home. Implementing this process can really help inform where to place which plant guilds, or even the designing of particular guilds to promote efficiency in the home.

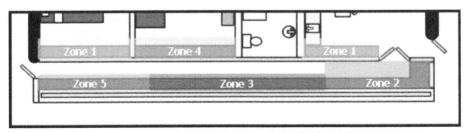

A double greenhouse layout labeled with zones.

Let's look at the image. The zones are highlighted and numbered one through five, denoting the frequency of visits and time spent in each location—one being the most frequent and five being the least. If we were going to design zone one in the kitchen/living room area on the upper right of the image, factoring in the other data gathered from processes in this chapter, what could or would be ideal in this area? Practical and efficient use of this planter space could be installing a commonly used culinary-herb-only guild near the kitchen, making access to the herbs easier, instead of having to run around the greenhouse to collect various herbs whenever it comes to meal prep time. Also, that microclimate is well-balanced, allowing the plants to be sustained throughout the year with a possible burst of growth during the winter, when the sun pushes deeper into the structure.

Another example could be for zone five, on the left side of the image, in the main greenhouse. Since this zone is visited the least, it would be practical to install a low-maintenance plant guild that does not require much attention at all, thereby significantly reducing wasted travel time to and fro.

Something else to consider during the design phase is how valuable a dedicated space for starting seeds, storing tools, pots, and things would be for you. There are a variety of reasons why some people may choose to have this in the greenhouse or not, but, in some shape or form, everyone will need it. If you do implement a nursery staging and storage area in the greenhouse, it may change the organization of your zones.

Plant to Cell Placement

As a caveat to zones and microclimates, including greywater planters to your Earthship or greenhouse adds another layer to your design considerations.

Many plant roots will do evasive measures to avoid greywater—having their roots spread laterally in the soil instead of plunging vertically down into the water. This behavior can lead to weak growth and overcrowding in the planter. Moreover, not all plants can even tolerate having saturated roots in first-use clean water, let alone greywater. If a plant with those particular sensitivities is in the wrong area, it will adversely affect the plant's health and ultimately lead to death. This process can be slow and frustrating for the greenhouse manager—to watch plants weaken steadily over time. Furthermore, it creates an increased vulnerability to pests, and is a surefire guarantee that more pest pressure will arise.

When working with greywater, especially, it is fundamental to ensure the correct type of plant gets placed in the proper location. The orientation of the greywater planters, with respect to the microclimates of the greenhouse, can significantly improve or weaken the performance of the system as well. If you currently have a greywater system in your greenhouse, be sure to identify microclimates (like full-sun) that will facilitate speedy processing and absorption of the greywater, and install plants that can best clean or reuse the greywater at that location. If you have the option to design the greywater system for your greenhouse, plan around the expected microclimates that will form so that the higher-flow greywater areas are in the best spot to avoid stagnation. Also, be sure to do some investigating beforehand on the particular needs that plants have concerning their placement within the system.

MAXIMUM GROW SPACE
UTILIZATION

When analyzing a current greenhouse setup or designing a new system, consider how to fill any voids or utilize un-used space. Guild designs can accomplish this through productive plant combinations and layering within single areas of the planter. This principle of maximizing grow space is an extension of that idea—to weave the entire greenhouse into a productive, cohesive whole so that all the individual guilds and microclimates begin to bind together as a unit. This chapter will highlight some options to help unify all the sections of the planter, while stacking as many yields as possible into the garden.

HANGING PLANTERS

Hanging planters serve to fill a gap that emerges between sets of guilds in the layout of the greenhouse. Each guild, when designed in the manner described above, will create a pocket of vertical space as it overlaps into the next. This pocket can effectively be used to hang small-to medium-sized pots. There are many creative options to choose from, and this part of the design process can be enjoyable and rewarding. The container type, hanging cord material, and how you construct it will be up to you. For example, my wife and I have been using old soup pots, colanders, and unique glass vases found inexpensively at local thrift shops as our hanging planters.

If you are up for some more hands-on work and attention, hanging planters are a great way to squeeze in extra production in the greenhouse. As a general expectation, if you grow primarily annual plants in these, you can plan to redo them on a three-to-four-month cycle. Most of the annual plants, by this time, will have reached maturity and produced the bulk of what they will, but once they begin to slow down and decline, they naturally become disease and pest vectors. Since the hanging planters are only loosely associated with the plant guilds and not in direct connection to the planter soil community, you run an even higher risk of pest and disease pressure emerging, because the soil biome cannot digest them in a normal fashion. Therefore, the role of the greenhouse manager here is to intervene and cut the life cycle of the annual short so that it can compost optimally.

Once the plant is cut down, you could either lay it on the topsoil as mulch to be processed or take it outside to a compost pile. In my opinion, it is wise to err on the conservative side here. Even if a plant is still producing a small amount, but its overall vigor is reduced, it is best to cut it down and compost it earlier rather than later. With proper planning, it should be no problem to have a healthy seedling take its place once the hanging planter is cleaned and ready to be rehung. There are always exceptions to the rule, and the greenhouse manager needs to observe and make the best call given the situation. Some plants are extra healthy and robust, living double the usual time. Others will be weak and frail, growing well for only half the average timespan. It is up to the discretion of the manager to cull or keep the plant.

Overall, when incorporating hanging planters, you can expect a bit more upkeep. There are plants, however, like lemongrass and basils, that can grow for very extended periods in the hanging planters with proper pruning maintenance. Researching and incorporating plants like these can reduce the total amount of work that goes into the hanging planters.

When it comes time to plant, seasonal appropriateness applies to plant selection. The closer you can approximate the natural growing rhythm of what the plants prefer, the better. Start your seedlings so that when it comes time to redo some buckets, the plants that like to grow in that season will be ready to go. For example, start your tomatoes in early spring, so when the buckets get turned over for the summer batch they can go in right away. In a later chapter, you will see in more depth how a cycle of seeding new plants, cutting down hanging planters, and cleaning them for replanting develops organically. There will be recommendations for which plants to propagate in the hanging planters for each season as well.

The Earthship Visitor Center has been a primary structure to showcase food production in Earthships. Since around 2012, the center has used translucent five-gallon buckets from the local hardware store with heavy-duty coated jute cord as the primary hanging planter containers. As you will see, these function like a wicking bed, which also mirrors the Earthship greywater planters in a smaller form. These buckets provide no drainage, which makes them uniquely suited to drier climates where evaporation rates and water usage is a challenge. They are also an excellent way to reduce the amount of potting mix needed per planter, because roughly half of the substrate is reusable indefinitely.

To start building the bucket, drill small holes near the top on opposing sides, and then thread the cord through, allowing enough slack for it to hang at the appropriate height. The bottom of the bucket is filled forty to sixty percent with a hydroponic media such as expanded clay pellets. Be sure to wash the media thoroughly before first use and before any subsequent reuse. A two-inch-wide PVC sight tube is cut to be the length of the bucket from bottom to the top. Nestle the tube into the media along the edge of the bucket. On top of the media and around the sight tube, apply a thin layer of straw. Enough straw should be used to cover the hydroponic media fully, so it is not visible when looking down into the bucket, but not so much that it takes up more than an inch or two vertically.

The remaining space in the bucket is filled with a potting mix. Make sure to keep the soil out of the sight tube. A small seedling or two can be planted out into the bucket then, and top-watered until large enough for its roots to reach the hydroponic media. Once the plants are a sufficient size, watering should take place via the sight tube. Pour the water down the pipe to fill about half the level of the bucket. Allow the plants to consume the water completely before rewatering. This system of filling and draining allows the plant's roots to get sufficient aeration before becoming submerged again.

It is imperative to monitor the water level, because it is easy to overwater with this method, which will drown the plants. Use the sight tube to monitor water levels if your bucket is opaque. Depending on the time of year and water needs of various plants, this style of hanging planter takes some getting used to, compared to conventional pots that drain out of the bottom. In the summer, some plants may need to be topped up with water twice a day, depending on the stage of growth and how much biomass is needed for support. In wintertime, generally, plant metabolism slows down, and you may only need to water a hanging planter like this once every few days, or only fill the planter up a quarter of the way instead of half.

A profile view of an evapotranspiration bucket.

Another aspect to consider when using this of style hanging planter is the nutrient source. Some form of liquid nutrient from either compost tea, store-bought fertilizer, or another type of organic fertilizer will be necessary to sustain the plants during growth (more on nutrient systems is in the Holistic Greenhouse Techniques chapter).

This method is possible with nearly any pot by plugging up any drainage holes and using macrame techniques to hang a container with no gaps or clips for hanging. By no means is it necessary to incorporate a hanging planter in this way. It is presented here to provide a window into the Earthship method and to offer a potentially useful alternative to more conventional practices. Using terracotta pots filled with potting mix will work just fine, allowing the excess water to drain onto the topsoil of the planter, if that is more appealing.

MUSHROOM LOGS

Shiitake mushrooms fruiting on logs.

A brief overview of mushrooms is the best place to start here so that we have a framework to understand what is possible and what to expect in the whole process within the greenhouse. There are three overarching types of mushrooms, based on their role and function in nature—mycorrhizal, parasitic, and saprophytic. Mycorrhizal species form symbiotic relationships with plant roots that constructively exchange nutrients and resources. Parasitic mushrooms do what they sound like they would—use living organisms as hosts to extract sustenance in an unequal exchange to grow and survive. The third type, saprophytic mushrooms, are primary and secondary decomposers. They live in dead and decaying organic material which they digest for food.

This third type is the best type for greenhouse cultivation, and most of the ideal varieties prefer decaying hardwood trees as their food and substrate. Some very skilled and experienced mycologists may be able to cultivate mycorrhizal mushrooms in the greenhouse space, but that is beyond the scope of this section. So, we will focus predominantly on saprophytic species and how to work with them.

The most suitable way to produce mushrooms in the greenhouse is via log or stump cultivation. Start by harvesting some fresh living hardwood logs or stumps in your local area, preferably in fall or winter. During this time of year, the wood is a denser food source for the mushrooms, because more sugars and nutrients are in the lower parts of the tree instead of the leaves or fruit. When harvesting logs or stumps, make sure to collect pieces that are at least five inches in diameter and a couple of feet long so that the yield will be worth the labor and time.

Oyster mushrooms fruiting on a stump.

Another critical point to note is that the harvested logs must be alive when you cut them. The logs you collect cannot have been sitting around for a year or two, or even have been laying on the lawn for a month or so. The reason for not collecting old logs is that a mushroom species will have already colonized them, and if you attempt to spawn those logs it will only create competition between the two species, most likely resulting in neither mushroom being able to fruit. Once you have the wood, it will need to rest for a couple of weeks away from direct soil contact. Resting the logs in this way prevents any other mushrooms from attempting to colonize it. After the antifungal forces in the wood dissipate, you can colonize with your desired strain.

Next, you need to acquire some mushroom spawn and basic items to get ready to inoculate the logs. Spawn and specialty mushroom cultivation items are available affordably online. See the Annotated Resource section at the end for some recommended suppliers of mushroom-growing materials. You will need a rubber mallet for spawn in the form of dowels, or a spawn plunger for loose spawn in grow material, a drill with a drill bit set, a pair of gloves, a small brush, and some food-grade wax, such as beeswax. The wax is used to seal the holes made in the wood, which helps deter pests and disease as well as lock in moisture.

Once the wood is ready and you have all the materials needed, sterilize your tools and create a clean workspace. If you have multiple strains of mushrooms that you plan to grow, only work with one at a time, because cross-contamination within the logs via your tools, or accidentally inoculating two types of mushrooms in one log, will cause competition in the substrate and lead to neither mushroom fruiting.

Inoculating logs and stumps differs slightly. In the case of a log, take your drill, equipped with a bit that matches the spawn plug size or plunger size, and drill a series of holes all around the bark in a diamond pattern. Only drill into the log enough so that the length of a dowel fits snugly, no more than a couple of inches. Then, take your plugs or plunger and fill all the holes, using a rubber mallet to gently tap any stubborn plugs fully into the log if you are using dowels. Once all the holes are filled, heat the wax in a bowl and use the small brush to seal the tops of the holes. Then, use the brush and wax to seal either end of the log.

When inoculating a stump, you follow a similar process, but do not drill into the bark. Instead, drill around the thinner ring between the bark and the larger inner circle of the exposed ends of the stump. This thinner outer ring is the sapwood, and the larger center ring is the heartwood. Inoculating the spawn in the sapwood helps to expedite the colonization stage. Once the spawn is in the holes, follow the same steps in sealing the ends with wax.

Once the logs or stumps are spawned and sealed, place them in a shadier zone of the planter. Be sure to elevate them slightly, away from direct soil contact with stones or a water-draining dish. Raising logs off the ground helps keep any other mushrooms from attempting to colonize them and discourages pests from attacking. The total colonization stage can take six months or more, depending on the size of the wood.

The job of the greenhouse manager during this period is to maintain the right growing conditions for the mushrooms in the wood. Optimal conditions are in a warm, shady zone with occasional watering, but nothing too excessive. Once the mushrooms have run out of substrate to continue to expand into, you will see some white patches forming at the ends of the wood. It has reached full colonization and you can initiate fruiting. There are several methods to promote fruiting; the best depends on the type of mushroom you are growing. The one widely used for the popularly cultivated varieties, and that I have the most experience with, is submerging the wood in water for twenty-four hours, simulating a heavy rain and giving the mushrooms the impetus to fruit. You could use a fifty-five-gallon drum, a cistern, or even a bathtub to accomplish this process.

Afterward, place the wood back in the designated spot in the planter and wait for the fruit to emerge. When the fruits are the ideal size, you can harvest them. Then, the mushrooms will need a recharging period, anywhere from a few weeks to a couple of months, depending on the log size and mushroom strain vigor, before you attempt to initiate another fruiting. The general rule of thumb for the time a log or stump will produce is: the diameter of the exposed end in inches equals years of productivity. For example, a log end that is five inches in diameter will produce mushrooms for five years. The length of fruiting duration may vary depending on the strain and wood quality as well.

BIOTYPOLOGY

A useful tool in your greenhouse design arsenal is an observational skill for identifying natural forms and utilizing their strengths to your advantage. Identifying biotypes stems and is adapted from the works of numerous homeopathic practitioners and researchers. In this section, we will highlight the most suitable biotypes of plants and seeds, as there is a wide range found in homeopathic literature. See the resource section for more information.

At first glance, this may seem to have little relevance, but an understanding of biotypology can be a powerful asset to promote health and balance in your greenhouse. Learning these forms and their implications will aid you in strategic seed selection, as well as plant placement. The basic portion presented here does not require extensive previous knowledge in the field of homeopathy to be useful.

Five biotypes are pertinent in identifying organic forms. They are sulphuric, carbonic, phosphoric, fluoric, and silic. These correlate to the natural elements of sulphur, calcium carbonate, phosphorus, fluorine, and silica. Starting sequentially with sulphur, then following down to silica, they are considered to be tiered levels of health. The sulphuric biotype is seen as the highest degree of health; the silic the least robust. Understanding the pathological health status is important to note, but each biotype fills its niche and can be used constructively to your advantage. Biotypes are not exclusive to particular plant families, genus or species, and any natural form can display any of the biotypes. The biotype that the seed reveals will carry through the plant's life. Plants of a particular biotype are not limited to reproducing its type, but all the biotypes are capable of emerging in the fruit and seed of the plant. For example, there could be five tomato plants in a garden, all of them grow out from seeds of the same fruit, and each one displays a different biotype.

Another example could be a family with five children. The first child has a sulphuric biotype, the second a carbonic, the third a phosphoric, and so on. In many cases, though, the fruit and seeds created may predominantly reflect the parents' biotype, but it is not exclusive or a hard-and-fast rule. This same principle applies to humans, insects, fungi, plants, or any biological form.

The "model" constitution is associated with the sulphuric biotype. Plants with this biotype are healthy, strong, not too big, not too small, not too skinny, or not too fat. They have excellent resistance to environmental pressures, stable metabolic performance, symmetrical growth patterns, and are all around ideal. It is easy to identify a sulphuric biotype because of this. If you go to an orchard or anywhere with many of the same plants in a small area, there will be some that stand out as the most shapely and beautiful. Of course, everyone is always hoping to have all their plants in the garden be sulphuric, but this is not realistic or practical. It makes sense to us to label the sulphur type as the best and always strive to have all your plants be this biotype, but nature makes use of diversity and does not share the same judging criteria of what is valuable as we do. The sulphur biotype has its role, just as all the rest of them do. Our job is to mimic the way nature weaves each biotype into the continuous stream of growth and development. The same should be true in our greenhouse. All the biotypes should be present to some degree to most effectively model the workings of nature.

In many cases, an excellent annual plant with the sulphuric biotype is perfect because of the shorter lifespan and the promise of a good crop of fruits. When planning for larger and perennial plants, though, the sulphuric biotype might not be the best for the overall greenhouse system. The vigor of a larger perennial sulphuric plant may overwhelm and out-compete the other plants it is associated with, thereby diminishing the overall beneficial interplay they could have. You could also be creating more work for yourself via the need to frequently prune the plant to conform it into the greenhouse.

The next rung down on the ladder of health is the carbonic biotype. It is still very high on the spectrum, but due to a few potential challenges, it comes in second. Its larger size most notably characterizes it. Carbonic plants have a slower metabolism with increased resource consumption. They tend to widen and thicken, but still retain an even growth pattern. Resistances to environmental pressures are reliable, but they do not respond well to transplanting or excessive movement. Carbonic plants much prefer to stay stable and grounded once established. They are not ideal for hanging planters, which are prone to swing, decreasing resistances and potentially affecting the quality and amount of the crop yielded. If you plant a carbonic plant in a container, be sure that it will not be necessary to move it around a lot.

Although they tend to produce in abundance, carbonic plants require more attention through frequent watering and feeding. As stated before, each form has a niche. A shrubby carbonic herbaceous plant could be an excellent choice for the planter if you are looking for more expansion laterally versus vertically. An example of a constructive usage for this biotype is to plant a carbonic banana in a shady zone full of greywater. The banana will grow slow and wide, consuming large amounts of greywater, benefiting from any surplus nutrients it can absorb as well. The sulphuric biotype displays the most balanced and uniform growth of all the types, and the carbonic grows slow, steady, and wide.

Plants of the phosphoric biotype tend towards a more slender form, often creating a kind of "C" shape. This biotype is the stereotypical tall and thin constitution, which commonly emerges because of its growth pattern. The phosphoric has a surge of growth, and then it slowly tapers off. The pattern possibly will repeat itself depending on the type of plant and its lifespan. This growth behavior causes the plant to shoot up tall and thin, then creating a drooping effect which makes the "C" shape. This type still retains a uniform and pleasing overall appearance.

Phosphoric types are not as resource consuming as the carbonic, making them a sound choice to integrate into a heavy-feeding plant guild to reduce input demands. Plants with this biotype often suffer from "skeletal deficiencies" that cause a weakness in its ability to hold itself up properly. This biotype is much more sensitive and responsive to the environment overall. Any environmental pressures can impact the health of the plant significantly in one direction or the other, but this is especially the case with colder temperatures. Phosphoric biotypes are still a very healthy option to design with, but not as robust and durable as the two previous types. When planning in the greenhouse space with phosphoric plants, be aware of the possible extra height at mature size. This biotype is best used to stack more plants in the prime location of the planter, due to its thinner vertical profile. These plants thrive in greenhouse conditions, because an attentive greenhouse manager can buffer the extremes of the environment.

Usually, when gardeners pick the seedlings they are going to plant out, the ones with fluoric biotypes will be last on the list. This biotype suffers from internal and external stresses, which manifest in appearance. It displays stunted, asymmetrical growth, and often has some form of discoloration or tissue malformation. Metabolically, it struggles with nutrient uptake and assimilation. It is slow-growing, either making an "S" shape or growing well in one direction, only to splinter off, regrowing in an opposite path. This type is often overlooked and underappreciated. Contained within the less-than-aesthetically-pleasing shape, are a profound resilience and survivalistic impetus. This can be a great asset, if utilized wisely. Using a fluoric plant to produce seed is a smart way to introduce and climatize new plant varieties to the greenhouse. When planning to install a new species, instead of picking and planting out the healthiest, most perfect-looking plant, you could opt for the haggard-looking fluoric one.

It is important to distinguish between an authentic fluoric biotype and a plant that has been undernourished or just neglected. This is done through comparison with the surrounding plants. If they all look in rough shape, it is probably improper management of some kind. If the surrounding plants appear healthy and there are one or two frail, struggling plants, those are your fluoric plants. If planted out in your greenhouse, well cared for and allowed to go to seed, those seeds will have had genetically passed on inborn hardiness that will accelerate adaptogenic and acclimatizing qualities. Using fluoric plants in this way can produce more robust and rugged plants for your greenhouse in the long term.

On par with the beauty of the sulphuric biotype, the silic is a petite version in externals only. This biotype is ranked lowest in regards to health, even with its ideal external shape. This superficial rating is due to its increased fragility and sensitivities. The silic biotype has challenges in nearly every category—from metabolic processes, environmental resistances, immune and recovery responses, they all reflect a weakened constitution. The plant is very slow-growing, thin, and has reduced production in most cases. Susceptible and vulnerable to most negative influences, this biotype can be used to compound the effect of pest indicator species. Once you have found a plant species that has displayed a biological incompatibility with the soil biome of your greenhouse planter, you can cultivate and select the silic biotype of the plant to speed possible pest detection.

Alternatively, since the greenhouse is a sheltered environment fostering ideal growing conditions, a silic biotype of a larger plant that generally would not be possible to cultivate could be raised with proper care and attention. Of course, the selection would still be for plants that are potential candidates for the greenhouse already, but are borderline options due to size. For example, a silic biotype of a chestnut tree would be out of the question because it would still become enormous. A better illustration may be a pomegranate tree with a silic biotype. The tree would benefit from all the pampering and coziness of the greenhouse, while still growing very slowly and be easy to maintain. Using this biotype in that way would be more for diversity and novelty, because of the reduced flowering and fruiting ability rather than for high yields.

Developing this skill for identifying and designing with biotypes can help you better understand your successes and failures when working with the plants and inform many aspects of your greenhouse management. With practice, you can learn to utilize the planter space and the plants themselves better. Many people think they do not have a green thumb, but it may just be a case of working with some plants that have a less than ideal biotype for their goals. Taking the time to examine the seeds you plant beforehand and identify their biotypes can help you select the best biotypes of that plant and know which biotypes of other plants it would combine well with to best share the space. This process can also help you set realistic expectations for plants in terms of their growth size and style, as well as the ways you can best assist their needs.

Sulphuric

Carbonic

Phosphoric

Flouric

Silic

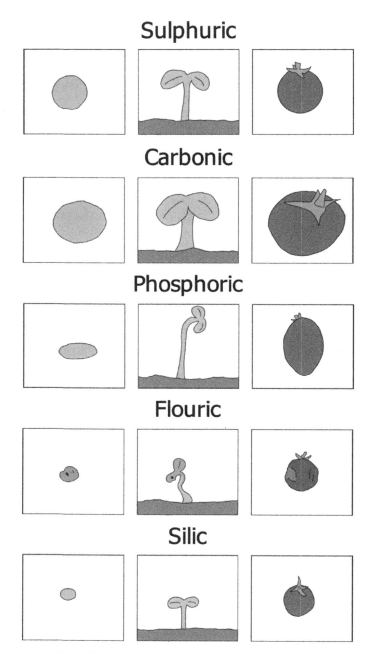

A chart that illustrates each biotype in seed, sprout and fruit form.

CHAPTER IV

HOLISTIC GREENHOUSE TECHNIQUES

In the previous chapter, we covered design components and layout considerations. Now, it is time to examine an array of practices and techniques for interfacing with the greenhouse system after the design phase, to promote balance and engender health. This chapter covers a range of options available to the greenhouse manager, all stemming from a holistic orientation. More conventional, modern modes of working with your greenhouse will not be included here because there are ample resources available elsewhere. The goal here is to become familiar with the operation and function of each option presented as well as discern which techniques would suit your greenhouse management style.

MULCH & MANAGEMENT STYLE

To mulch or not to mulch, that is the question. There comes a time in every greenhouse gardener's life when one must decide. Holistic management styles are achievable by any of the options presented here or by a combination thereof. This choice sets the framework for your management style. There are undoubtedly other aspects that will play into it, but this decision is fundamental to how you end up interfacing with your greenhouse and which tools and practices you utilize and when. These management styles are inherently no-till systems, but in some scenarios, a greenhouse manager may choose to run a tillage system. In this section, the only form of "tillage" performed will be when digging a small hole to transplant a seedling. In my opinion, tilling the soil becomes counterproductive to running a holistic operation and will be omitted from this book. For those of you who find the options presented here unsuitable, the resource section contains some links to other books that utilize milder forms of till systems, such as broadforking, for your convenience.

The element of mulching can affect many facets of your greenhouse management style, from how you utilize specific resources to the amount of time involved in certain tasks, and to overall aesthetics and systemic health. All the options require an effort to maintain harmonious conditions in the greenhouse, directed in different ways, and making use of different techniques at different times. Some aspects may become easier, while posing possible challenges in other areas. If you have not given this topic much thought, be sure to meditate on it well, because it is a crucial decision. To truly get a full understanding of the impact and scope of this choice, the content of this chapter needs to be digested and processed in conjunction with the needs and goals of your situation. Some things may be doubled up on, and others taken away to optimize your greenhouse management style.

No-Mulch

Greenhouse managers who choose not to mulch the top-soil can achieve a more conventional groomed garden appeal. If well kept, the results of a no-mulch greenhouse can be truly stunning and highly productive, but it will undoubtedly demand care. Three aspects cause this style to require more up-keep and attention than others—consistent pruning and dead-heading, frequent visits to the composting area to deposit material, and increased top watering of the planter.

Consistent pruning and deadheading stimulates the health of the plants and also aids in buffering disease and pest pressure if done correctly. In this method, apply all decaying material to the compost located outside of the greenhouse, instead of allowing it to build up and cover the soil or remain for any significant period on the plant itself. In this way, you transfer the normal recycling process of nature from the interior to the exterior to keep the greenhouse as free as possible from forces of decomposition, and promote the plants within to remain in their prime growth and maturity stage.

Since the majority of the decomposition process takes place outside the greenhouse, the scraps of organic material collected will need to find good use there. If you plan to manage your greenhouse with no-mulching, I strongly advise reviewing the "Turn Bin" composting section. I recommend this method of composting for no-mulch setups because it produces a size-able portion of usable end product more quickly than other methods. A faster compost turnover will allow you to have a more regular stream of humus to spread on the topsoil, which replenishes nutrients and stimulates biological activity. Keep in mind that composting in this way will continue to add to the time and labor of running a healthy greenhouse because the turn bin method requires the most upkeep and attention of the composting styles outlined in this chapter.

Another consideration is water consumption. A no-mulch system will be comparatively less water-efficient overall than its alternatives. Without the use of mulch, there is lower moisture retention in the soil, so manually watering will be increased compared to other systems. This dependence on frequent top watering ultimately affects the total system resilience. The greenhouse could become hyper-dependent upon the greenhouse manager during peak season, in which case you cannot miss a beat or the plants will quickly suffer.

Sun damage to the topsoil is another element that plays into the amount of top watering that is necessary. If the topsoil is left to get too dry, all the time you have invested in cultivating a healthy soil community can be significantly set back by killing off the biological constituents found there. Executing flawless manual watering can become a slippery slope if the greenhouse becomes too neglected, and overall, it can become a delicate balancing act to maintain a robust and happy greenhouse.

The Earthship Visitor Center in Taos is a prime example of this style of management. It is unique because it is a showcase building that needs to be in a constant state of beauty and health to best illustrate what is possible in an Earthship greenhouse to visitors. At all times of year, this greenhouse needs to be attractive, appealing, and presentable to the general public. So, it is perfectly adapted as a no-mulch system, because these greenhouses are the most aesthetically familiar to the broadest range of people, and have the tidiest appearance, compared to the other styles.

For people who have the time and drive to dedicate, this method may be no problem at all; but for others, it may become an overbearing chore. If there may be increased foot traffic through the greenhouse and having a wow factor is a consideration, this style may be for you. So, if you do not mind more time grooming the plants, dedicating the bulk of your finished compost to replenishing the topsoil, and top watering more often, then no-mulching could be an ideal and rewarding choice.

Mono-Mulch

This style offers a bit of each of the other options. Mono-mulching allows you to maintain a reasonably well-kept greenhouse appearance, co-opt more biological forces in the rhizosphere, retain more moisture, and slowly build topsoil. In regards to upkeep and time, mono-mulching is a middle ground between no-mulch and poly-mulch. As the name implies, it utilizes only a single type of mulch in the planters, so, it is imperative to source quality material. The mulch material can be something like hardwood chips, straw, or leaves. If planning to use wood chips, make sure to avoid the colored mulches at hardware stores. These bagged mulches contain dyes to achieve a pleasing color to the eye, but are a hindrance to the soil biology. To chip your own wood would undoubtedly be ideal, because you could check the health level of the wood before you chip it and guarantee what is going into your greenhouse is a good product.

If you choose to use straw, be aware of the source and the farming practices used to produce it. Sometimes it be can difficult to get a clear answer about this, because most stores are not asked that question and won't bother to find out, or it may be too complicated for them because it comes from multiple sources. The reason it is so important is that some farmers use burndown chemicals like glyphosate (as in RoundUp) on their soils and crops, which can accumulate in the straw and be very adverse to the functioning of a holistic program. The same is true for leaves or any mulch material you decide to use. If you can source the materials from someone or somewhere you know and trust, that is the most surefire way to go.

In this system, cover any bare areas of soil with an inch-to-two-inch layer of clean quality mulch. You prune any dead or decaying material and remove it to an exterior compost pile, just like in a no-mulch system, but now you will have more composting styles to choose from. The variety of composting methods accessible to you is due to the decreased demand for refreshing the topsoil, compared to a no-mulch system. In a mono-mulch management style, the mulch slowly becomes topsoil over time, so you could opt for a compost setup that is less intensive and takes longer to produce a finished product. Once the compost pile is ready for application and the mulch has been digested into the soil, you apply a layer of fresh compost on top, and then top dress again with a new batch of mulch. Following this pattern and repeating this cycle over a longer time frame decreases the overall work and input time in the greenhouse, while upholding and retaining fertility.

Another significant benefit to using this system over a no-mulch one is that using mulch expands the diversity of the biological community in the soil. It creates a complete reflection of natural processes, while still being easily manageable. Having mulch supports the incorporation of saprophytic mushrooms, which can produce an edible yield if the right species colonize the mulch. Even if they are not edible, these mushrooms help with overall soil strength, ward against erosion, make more nutrients available in the soil, and aid in water retention. With this quantity of mulch, you will also be employing some smaller shredding and chopping insects, without being too inviting to larger critters trying to work their way into the greenhouse. The smaller insects in the rhizosphere will help break down the mulch and also help balance pest populations. These are all significant advantages that are hard to replicate and contribute to eliminating unnecessary pressures on the greenhouse manager.

Just as the mushrooms colonizing the mulch help with moisture retention, the mulch itself stores water and helps consistently keep the soil hydrated. This extra hydration protects the garden from drying out too quickly, giving the greenhouse manager more freedom from intensive top watering. With a mulch covering, no direct sun rays are damaging the topsoil, allowing the soil community to flourish unhindered, promoting better nutrient exchange.

After a couple of seasons with an alternate management style, you could always adopt this method. Switching between any of the management styles works, so you can try them all out and see which is best for your lifestyle and needs. Mono-mulching will most likely be the best choice for the broadest range of people, as it requires a moderate amount of attention, but still creates an attractive and beautiful space throughout the entire year.

Poly-Mulch

The underlying function and operation of these three styles is the degree to which the greenhouse manager allows composting action to take place within the greenhouse system itself. The no-mulch system allows the least amount of composting to take place in the greenhouse, and in turn, increases the total workload for the gardener. Mono-mulching is the median in regards to both composting action and workload. Last, but not least, the poly-mulching style allows the maximum amount of composting action to take place within the greenhouse and requires the least amount of energy. The poly-mulching method offers all the benefits of mono-mulching with even more reduced demand on replenishing the topsoil, allowing more freedom and versatility for applying nutritional program techniques. The downsides of this style are an overall messier appearance, periodical reductions in total biomass (which can also play into a less than desirable appearance), and increased risk of pest expansion.

This method is a perpetual mulching cycle that never uncovers the soil and recycles the dead and decaying organic material produced by the greenhouse directly within the greenhouse itself. Whatever clippings come from the plants get applied directly to the topsoil as mulch, excluding only very diseased or pest-infested material. Placing all the organic material from the greenhouse onto the topsoil leads to mulch of all shapes and sizes and in varying stages of decomposition. To many it may look like an eyesore, but to others it may be beautiful. Although it may take some getting used to, it builds up the armor on the soil with a smorgasbord of different nutrients that, in turn, creates a health-bolstering effect in the greenhouse.

The foundation for success with this style lies in caring for and cultivating a robust soil biome, capable of digesting organic material quickly and efficiently. Providing a diverse and nutritious diet to the soil community is essential. It is practical to manage this system by growing your mulch to chop and drop directly in and onto the planter. Instead of any bare areas of the soil initially being covered with a type of mulch or left exposed, you grow a combination of plants that can easily undergo termination during their flowering period to then cover the soil—repeating this process over and over with different plants for different seasons. With this system, at all times, you have both a living mulch which aids in nutrient cycling and biodiversity in the greenhouse, as well as decaying mulch from the previously chopped combination of plants grown in that spot. See the "multi-species cover crop" section of this chapter for a more in-depth explanation of the mechanics of growing your mulch.

The downside to this process is mainly aesthetic. Your greenhouse will alternate between times of hearty and vibrant biomass and periods of empty, scraggly, messy-looking planters. For some, this may be a deal breaker; for others, an exciting prospect. It all depends on individual preferences.

As far as what is allowed to take part in the decomposition cycle, there is a definite line to draw when it comes to Earthship greenhouse management. This line may be stretched to some degree if the greenhouse is not attached to the home, but even so, the boundary lines will be similar. The greenhouse is fundamentally a division from nature, and no one would want to host the full spectrum of animals, insects, bacteria, fungi, and weather conditions that take part in the normal uncontrolled decomposition cycle the natural world performs. For example, nobody would want a smelly rotting cabbage, rodents, or lots of mold in their greenhouse, and that would not be conducive to a genuinely healthy system anyway. Therefore kitchen scraps cannot be added directly to the soil because of the smell and attractiveness to large and small critters. These items will continue to be composted outdoors or in worm bins (see the vermiculture section for more details on this practice).

The bulk of the work in the poly-mulch system lies in the well-timed termination of cover crops and effective use of techniques like holistic sprays or compost teas. Whether you succeed or fail with this style starts and ends with the soil. When the rhizosphere is diverse and active, it will filter up through the rest of the greenhouse, helping to create equilibrium and health. If the biological engine of this system becomes weak, slow, polluted, or compromised somehow, then pests can and will easily overtake the system, which can be a nightmare. If this decline begins to happen, the pests that inhabit the greenhouse will muster their forces to take down all the frail plants quickly. Much to the dismay of many, this is a normal function in nature. These insects are merely doing their job as biofilters for the food chain, preventing plants that are unsuitable to continue to proliferate. Poly-mulching systems are laxer, when it comes to the presence of common pests in the greenhouse, because there is more insect activity overall helping to check populations. This increased insect activity is not extreme, but could be another deal-breaker for many.

Poly-mulching greenhouses can teeter on the edge of looking too wild and messy, with extra insects floating around and random plants popping up everywhere, but with some practice and skill, this style can produce the most consistently diverse yields. This style may be ideal for the home gardener who does not mind not having a constant well-kept appearance and enjoys a wider variety of plants in the greenhouse throughout the year.

Mixed Management Style

The three management styles presented here constitute the fundamental modes of operating a greenhouse. While each one can function independently and produce excellent results, once you feel comfortable with these systems, there is potential to integrate elements of each type into a customized management style uniquely adapted to you. As you develop your particular style and get to know the specialties of your greenhouse, the adjustments more suited to you will most likely naturally become apparent. For example, let us take a mono-mulched greenhouse in which the mulch layer is allowed to decompose throughout the year before re-application. Instead of following the standard mono-mulching protocol of applying a fresh coat of compost and top-dressing that with a layer of mulch, you could work a multi-species cover crop blend into the compost layer, and then mulch on top of that. In effect, this would produce a hybrid mono-mulch system with a single multi-species cover crop blend added to the annual cycle, but would not be as intensive as two or three cover crop rounds per year as in a poly-mulch based greenhouse.

Another adaptation would be the use of certain ground covers to act as living mulch. Adding a fulltime ground cover could provide a more consistent and cohesive networking ability for the soil biome and cut down on the number of seasonal tasks. Incorporating living mulches into a no-mulch management style can significantly improve the health of the greenhouse. It will reduce water loss during the warmer seasons, increase fertility, and help cut down on the frequency of maintenance. The gradual combination of customizations into your management style like these is possible. Adapting your style over time could ultimately end up in creating an even more robust and healthy greenhouse system and provide a much more dynamic and exciting set of yields from season to season.

COMPOST & COMPOST STYLES

Composting is a ubiquitous primordial activity that is foundational in the natural world for the breakdown and recycling of dead or decaying organic matter. During various stages of the composting process, a myriad of biological forces aids in the transmutation of organic material into a living nutrient-rich product called humus. This natural process has been espoused on a human scale for ages and is a tried and true agricultural tool.

The composting process is broken up into four identifiable phases—mesophilic, thermophilic, cooling, and curing. During the mesophilic phase, the compost heap reaches temperatures between 50 and 113 degrees Fahrenheit, and in this range, a particular set of organisms thrive. In the thermophilic stage, compost temperatures reach 113–158 degrees and promote another set of organisms that thrive and facilitate the composting activity. In the cooling phase, nearly all the compost material has gone through thorough digestion, processing, and conversion into humus. The temperatures then slowly drop, allowing for the establishment of a more stable biological community. The curing phase allows the humus to mature into the best end product possible. In the various composting styles presented here, these phases generally overlap into one another rather than being distinctly separate.

For the composting process to produce quality humus, several requirements need to remain in balance, as with any living being,—moisture, air, warmth, and food. The compost pile needs to remain moist, but not too wet or too dry. If it becomes too wet or dry, it will kill the living inhabitants performing all the work, and the composting process will cease. If there is a lack of air, anaerobic conditions emerge, which will ultimately break down the material. Employing aerobic forces will produce a higher quality finished product. If the environment becomes too hot or too cold, the compost community will slow down, and if extreme enough, will die. Finally, all the residents and elements of the heap need an adequate diversity of organic material textures and nutrients, a ratio of dry to fresh materials.

In my climate, I aim for a ratio of three parts of dry material to one part of fresh. Learning the harmony of this recipe is best done hands-on, as it quickly becomes intuitive and second nature with a little experience. It is also worthy to note that for any of the styles presented here, aside from vermiculture, it is best to add any harder soil amendments into the piles during the composting period, not top-dress afterward. Mixing the amendments into the compost allows for better integration and homogenization with the soil biome, making the amendments more accessible overall.

It is vital to have a solid understanding of the mechanics and uses of compost because clean, healthy, and well-made compost is an essential ingredient in running a successful holistic greenhouse. We will cover a few different options of composting styles, including a basic procedure for each. There are many diverse methods beyond what is presented here to integrate composting into a health regimen for your greenhouse. The four selected for this chapter represent a balance of variety to illustrate some viable possibilities. What will best suit you depends on the volume of organic material generated on your site, the inputs for the compost pile based on your diet, as well as your climate and the time you are willing to dedicate to the process.

TURN BINS

A turn bin composting setup is a series of small-to-medium-sized compartments set up laterally against one another. Each compartment or "bin" is uniform in size, and ideally no larger than a 5-foot-by-5-foot square and no smaller than a 3-foot-by-3-foot square. These dimensions allow for the piles to fully facilitate every stage of composting while still being manageable with hand tools. The dividing walls that separate the bins should be about knee height and no higher, as this would increase the difficulty of the turning process. The amount and frequency of compost material generated within the home dictate the size of the bins. The more material made on site, the larger the bins can be or the higher the number of total bins in the system. Each compartment that contains a pile is covered with a small tarp or plastic sheet to prevent water loss and block direct sunlight, which would slow the composting process.

The turn bin method is the most energy/labor intensive method because it requires manually transferring piles from one compartment to another with a pitchfork. Turning the piles should be done at reasonably regular intervals, like once a week, depending on the season. The purpose of this process is to monitor temperature, increase aeration, and ensure uniformity in the breakdown and composting of all the material in a pile. These things are essential for the quality of the end product. If the compost heats up too much, there will be significant nutrient loss. Through aerating the pile during the turning process, you can guarantee that no dead zones form, and aeration also promotes increased bacterial action, which speeds the breakdown process. Besides, turning provides the ability to give all the organic material multiple opportunities to be in direct contact with the most active part of the pile, as well as ensure that all areas of the pile retain balanced ratios, conducive to continuing a healthy composting activity.

The Earthship Biotecture Visitor Center, a showcase building for food production, uses a five-bin turn system for composting. This breaks down into three active piles—a mesophilic, a thermophilic, and a cooling pile—one empty bin for turning, and one curing pile (which does not get turned) at all times. You could orient the piles in the opposite way, but for this explanation, as you face the composting bins, the left-most pile is where you deposit the fresh compost. This bin is generally in the mesophilic phase because of the continuous additions of fresh material. The next compartment to the right will be in a thermophilic phase, and the bin to the right of that will be in the cooling phase. The empty bin will alternate to either end of the active piles, depending on which way the bins can move. So, if there is an empty bin to the left of the freshest (mesophilic) pile, every bin would then get turned one bin to the left. If the empty bin is to the right of the cooling pile, then each bin gets turned over one bin to the right.

The frequency in which this should happen is, ideally, once a week. When turning the active piles with the pitchfork, be sure to do two things. One, make the outer portions of each pile, which have less composting activity taking place than the center, become the center of the pile as you turn it to ensure that it gets a period of increased composting action. Second, shake and break open clumps that form as you transfer the material into the other bin. Taking time to open up clusters promotes the most aeration possible throughout the whole pile.

Once the cooling pile is ready to transfer into the curing bin, you will need to buy or build a sifting screen. It can be as simple as four two-by-fours drilled together in a square, with a half-inch-mesh screen attached across the frame. Then, place the sifter over the curing bin. Take a pitchfork or shovel and transfer the cooling pile onto the screen, a couple of shovelfuls at a time, then shake and massage the compost through the screen down into the curing bin. The pieces that are too big to fit through the sifter and not fully composted yet can then be placed into the leftmost (mesophilic) pile to run through the composting process again. Continue this until the cooling pile is entirely deposited into the curing box and cover it with a tarp.

Next, turn the thermophilic pile, which would have been the middle pile, into the bin that the cooling pile was in, and the mesophilic pile into the bin that the thermophilic pile was in. Moving the piles in this way makes room to begin building a fresh new pile in the bin that the mesophilic pile was in. Since no more fresh compost scraps go into what was formerly the mesophilic pile, it will naturally proceed to the thermophilic stage, and the pile that was previously in the thermophilic phase can begin to enter the cooling phase.

Lastly, the new pile that is forming will take the place of the old mesophilic pile as it grows in size. So, the pattern of this composting style is as follows—harvest cured compost for use in the greenhouse, sift cooled compost into the curing bin, move the active piles over one bin, and start a new pile.

Building up a fresh pile is done in a layering fashion. Once a week, compost scraps from the Earthship or garden are collected and brought out to the composting area. Remove the tarp and distribute the fresh scraps evenly along the top of the pile. You can dump it all on top and use the pitchfork to spread it out. Then, add a good layer of straw, enough to cover the fresh scraps fully and block any unwanted smells from escaping on top. The pile can then be covered up again with the tarp. Be sure to always add fresh compost material to the leftmost (mesophilic) pile.

Adhering to this method can be repeated indefinitely and could potentially be an excellent fit in your seasonal greenhouse management routine. On the Earthship Biotecture grounds, this method produces a full wheelbarrow or two of cured compost every three to four months, excluding the winter season when it slows down significantly.

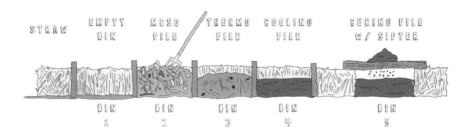

STRAW — EMPTY BIN — MESO PILE — THERMO PILE — COOLING PILE — CURING PILE W/ SIFTER

BIN 1 — BIN 2 — BIN 3 — BIN 4 — BIN 5

Though the turn bin system is the most consistently labor-intensive method outlined here, it allows for the most margin for error because you are regularly checking and modifying its condition. If you are new to composting, I recommend starting with this style, as it will give you a solid foundation and under-standing of the mechanics and stages. And, the faster overall time to completion of this style allows you to get a better grasp of the whole process more quickly than the other techniques, which can take well over a year, in some cases, to fully com-post. If you try this method for a few seasons to get a feel for how the system operates, you will have a better framework, increased proficiency, and more confidence for working with a more hands-off or intricate style. Then, when or if you decide to change your compost method, you will be better equipped to handle any challenges. Utilizing the finished compost in the greenhouse is covered in the subsequent sections.

NO TURN

No-Turn composting systems are simple, straightforward, and low-impact. This style produces a great final product, can easily handle larger volumes of organic material, and only requires a moderate amount of labor. The downside to this method is the total composting time for completion. Depending on the compost heap contents, no-turn can take up to a year to compost once the last material is on the pile. Although it is not mandatory to do so, no-turn composting is the only method here described that can compost human waste safely. This makes it suitable for the most radical folks who want to use a composting toilet instead of a flush one. This section will not dive extensively into that aspect, so look in the resource section for "The Humanure Handbook" for more information.

There are many sophisticated plans and designs available online for building a specialized composting area for this style. They include things like extra compartments for cover material, locking and removable slats for ease of access, and a roof with rain barrels to shade the compost and collect water for direct use in hydrating the pile. Until you are sure and have enough space for a more permanent composting area, I would recommend keeping it as low-tech and affordable as possible, so that it can be easily dismantled and relocated if need be. The need to dismantle and move the setup often becomes the case for gardens and landscape designs as they evolve, so I would only invest in constructing a composting area for very established residences. From my experience, a set of pallets drilled together to make a cube shape, with the front pallet being removable and the top open, works just perfectly. The total footprint when using pallets can be as small as a 5-foot cube with a covered straw bale next to it.

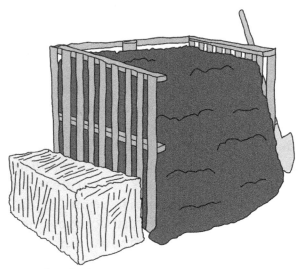

A simple low cost no-turn compost setup.

Once you have your designated composting area, you will need some cover material like straw or leaves, and a shovel or pitchfork. To build the pile, start with a base layer of cover material and deposit the organic material on top. Spread it out to fill the space with a pitchfork. Repeat this layering for the next few deposits until the pile is, evenly, about a foot high. Be sure to provide some extra straw on the top of each deposit to buffer sunlight from slowing the composting process and prevent water loss. The extra straw also helps to trap air, which is helpful because you will not be aerating it by turning the pile. Depending on your climate, you may want to shield the top of the pile by covering it with a tarp. This covering helps in wet climates to shed some unwanted rainfall and keep the pile from becoming too soggy.

For all subsequent compost material deposits, take the pitchfork, plunge it into the center of the pile and pull towards you to open a pocket in the middle. Then, dump the compost scraps into the center and apply a generous amount of cover material over the top. Always depositing the fresh scraps into the center ensures that every bit of compost gets to be in the hottest section of the pile for a decent amount of time, while maintaining the right ratio of material types. In no-turn composting systems, it is crucial to build the pile with proper layers as you deposit each new load of organic material, because it is increasingly difficult to correct that, as compared to the turn bin system, where it is relatively easy.

A sound investment for a pile of this type is a compost thermometer. This can give you a heads-up if the pile is not heating enough or heating up too much. You can adjust accordingly, by either adding something high in nitrogen to stimulate the compost, like alfalfa or chicken waste if the pile is not heating up, or use the pitchfork to break open the pile from the top a few times to let it breathe and cool. Another alternative to help with aeration and moderating temperature is possible if the pile is not used for composting human waste. As you build up the pile every one-half to one foot or so, lay a branch or pole at an angle on top of the pile, making sure it is long enough to protrude beyond each end. Then, continue to build the pile as usual on top of the branches or poles you inserted. When the pile starts to heat up beyond what is the optimal range, pull out a few of the branches or poles, allowing for heat to escape and providing deep aeration into the pile.

The no-turn method might be the best option for the greenhouse manager who does not have time to dedicate to dealing with the compost every week. The frequency of visits to this type of pile is regulated by how long it takes for your compost bin to fill up in the house. Which, in some cases, can be a month or more, depending on how much you cook and how many people live in the home. If you feel confident in your compost-pile-building abilities, and if you are not in a rush for cured compost, this method may be the way to go.

BIODYNAMIC

Most people have at least heard of the term biodynamic, whether they know the source of its creation and its practices or not. Many biodynamic farms have cropped up all over the world, with unique products and avenues of production. Some biodynamic farmers produce exclusively wines that have gained some notoriety. Other farms carry the biodynamic torch by attempting to evolve and develop more or different preparations. A full understanding of the biodynamic movement requires at least a foundational knowledge of some underlying anthroposophical worldviews and tenets. Anthroposophy is a term coined by Dr. Rudolf Steiner for the study of the wisdom of the human being. Unfortunately, this book is not the appropriate forum to go in depth into the topic, but as mentioned before, relevant links will be provided if this is something of interest for the reader.

The beginnings of the biodynamic farming movement were born out of a set of anthroposophical lectures on agriculture given by Dr. Steiner in the 1920s. Since then, it has continued to grow, now gaining widespread popularity in organic and sustainable circles. In this section, we will cover the basics of the standard biodynamic compost pile.

Biodynamic composting is more involved and specific than the other styles. It also requires a bit more experience and access to resources than the rest, but can yield a fantastic end product. Incorporating the full protocol of the biodynamic model works best for large-scale agricultural operations that can partition off a section of the finished compost for the greenhouse, or for homesteaders who have access to livestock. In biodynamics, there is a differentiation between the preparation of manure piles and regular composting piles. In general, the construction, layout, and process of both are very similar, but we will focus here on the standard compost pile, because it will be the most relevant to the broadest group of greenhouse gardeners.

The first notable feature is that of compost orientation and size. New piles are best placed on bare soil and built up from a small trench dug out with a shovel. As with all compost piles, a shady area is better than full sun. The dimensions for the standard biodynamic compost pile are 12 to 15 feet wide at the base, standing 5 to 7 feet tall, tapering up to 6 to 8 feet wide at the top. The shape of the pile is narrower at the top, sloping out and down to be wider at the bottom (see image). It somewhat resembles a large loaf of bread or Yule log cake. On top of the pile is a depression that runs along the center and allows for hydrating the pile efficiently. These dimensions can scaled up or down, as long as the proportions remain in the proper ratio. The span of piles can also be variable, running up to about 25 feet long if enough material is on site.

The next important element is the construction of the pile. It is built up in layers, just like the others. Starting with a base of straw at the bottom, build up with a layer of compost material a foot thick, then a thin layer of garden lime and/or mineral amendments, next, a segment of one to three inches of soil or peat, and then repeat this pattern until the pile has reached the appropriate height. Once the heap has taken the proper shape, it is sealed off all around with turf, peat, or a soil-like material. The pile can be built up incrementally, but if possible, it is ideal for constructing it all at once, so it can be capped off with an earthen substrate right away. If extreme weather conditions exist, it may need further shielding with some brush, straw, or leaves.

To fully adhere to the biodynamic process, once the pile has been built up satisfactorily and sealed off, six special preparations get inserted from the top of the pile about two feet deep inside. These preparations are made from several common plants, such as dandelion and yarrow, and have particular methods of compiling and processing. To learn more about these see the biodynamic compost preparations subsection, following this one, and also the resource section for links.

Once the pile is the correct shape and size, leave it alone to compost, aside from intermittently checking to ensure proper composting is taking place. You also want to occasionally water or fertilize with manure tea or something of that nature. At around month four or five, the pile should be sufficiently broken down, in which case take off the peat or soil covering and turn the pile over, mixing all the layers. It will continue to rest and cure for a few months following the turn. A standard time frame for this whole composting process is around eight to twelve months.

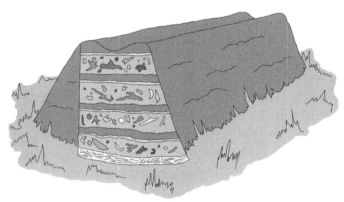

A profile view of a complete biodynamic compost pile.

As I said at the beginning of this section, this style is more involved and specific. Once you read through the next section on compost preparations, you will see that this is true. This style is best suited for small homestead operations or even large-scale ranches. On a small scale, it could be ideal for an avid biodynamic follower who is already familiar with the specialties that go into this composting method, or someone curious to experiment with something new.

BIODYNAMIC COMPOST PREPARATIONS

Nine preparations were put forth at the inception of the biodynamic movement and remain today as the core standard, even though biodynamics as a whole has continued to evolve. A number of these preparations called for animal parts or organs. Some people are put off by this, and others will not have access readily to the animal parts needed to complete the preparations. Another inhibiting factor may be that your climate does not host the particular plants required for the preparations. In that case, you would have to connect with a local biodynamic group to find out if they have developed any new or modified preparations for your area, or order some of the supplies from a biodynamic supplier online. These preparations can be very time-intensive, compared to other means of fertilization. Some of the compost preparations take a full year or more to obtain a completed product. So, these techniques may not be suitable for everyone.

The preparations fall in two groups— horn and compost, with the horsetail preparation being on its own. The two horn preparations are manure and silica. The six compost preparations are yarrow, chamomile, nettle, oak bark, dandelion, and valerian. The horn and horsetail preparations are in the liquid fertilizer section, as they are not specifically for the creation of compost but applied to the soil and plants. The compost preparations work as additives and stimulants for the compost pile, assisting significantly in the decomposition and breakdown process. Even if you choose not to build your compost pile in the biodynamic form, these preparations can be useful and their benefits conferred to whatever pile style you opt to make. In the remainder of this section, we will briefly spotlight each compost preparation.

The mission and scope of the biodynamic movement impact more than just agriculture. The movement is designed to address the particular needs of our time. Many people view the preparations as odd, and are often confused by the incorporation of animal parts. To attempt to shed some light on the reasoning behind this, I will summarize my understanding from studying biodynamic materials. The use of animal organs is an attempt to imbue an agricultural system with a form of residual animal impact, thereby engendering a more holistic reflection and imprint of how nature operates. It is, in effect, trying to fill in for the inputs of nature lost with the expansion of human civilization and industrial farming practices. Over time, our landscape and soils have become damaged, demineralized, and the influence of many wild ecological elements has been extinguished from our food production systems. The decline of biological complexity has led to a decline in the quality and health of both the produce and the land. The manifold niches that nature employs to create balance, harmony, and health are part of the regenerative process.

As we continue to strip away, simplify, and isolate our agricultural practices into monoculture-based systems, we stray from the patterns of nature. The use of organs in these preparations helps bridge the ever-increasing gap of biological purity and integrative methods in progressively fragmented and compromised landscapes. Since this book is not solely on the topic of biodynamics, my comments here on the intentions and principles of it only skim the surface of what the scope of this movement encapsulates. To fully absorb and understand what is put forth in this method of farming, it would be best to delve into it for yourself. See the resource section for several links.

Yarrow - *Achillea millefolium*

The yarrow preparation is one of the more complicated to

execute, due to the amount of time involved and the materials. In addition to needing a healthy portion of yarrow flowerheads, you will need one or more blown-up bladders from a male deer. Not everyone has a hunter in the family, and requesting a blown-up bladder out of a trophy kill from a family member may be unusual enough, let alone asking a stranger. Nevertheless, a puffed-up buck bladder is what this recipe calls for, and if you happen to be able to source this—however, you do—it is definitely worth giving this preparation a shot. To start, you need to harvest as much yarrow as you can find and adequately dry it as if you were going to use it as a tea. Store the dried yarrow flower heads for a year, during which time you need to acquire the stag bladder so it can be hung and air-dried. The following year, in the spring, you need to harvest more yarrow and make a fresh pressed juice from the plant, and use that juice to hydrate the yarrow flower heads dried from the previous year. At the same time, slightly rehydrate the bladder and then, as you can probably guess, stuff it full of the yarrow. Once stuffed with the flowerheads, the bladder will need to be tied and hung up in a sunny area, making sure to safeguard it from birds or other animals.

The bladder remains hung until fall, when it is taken down and buried in the ground and allowed to decompose fully. The construction for the burial pit looks something like this: It is dug out about 2 feet deep and large enough to accommodate however many stuffed bladders you have. The bottom is lined with some brush or lath screen to deter pests from attempting to eat them over the winter. A few inches of soil is placed over the top of the base brush layer. Place the bladder on top of the soil, keeping them evenly spaced if more than one. Cover again with a thin layer of soil and fill in any gaps. Next, lay a burlap sheet or sack of some kind over top to mark the boundary for where the bladder is, so that it does not incur damage during the excavation process. On top of the sack, lay some more brush and anything else you may have to deter animals from making their way into the pit.

The following spring, remove all the layers on top of the bladder and be careful not to disturb too much, because by then the bladder will most likely have fully broken down and harvesting the yarrow may become messy. Once you have collected the flowers, the preparation is complete and ready to be administered in the compost pile. As with all the compost preparations, when added to the pile, it acts as a stimulant to promote active decomposition, thus improving the speed and end quality of the finished compost.

Chamomile - *Matricaria recutita*

The chamomile preparation calls for, in addition to chamomile, the small intestine of a cow. It is affectionately known as the chamomile sausage preparation. Harvested flowerheads are dried in the same fashion as the yarrow previously described, then stored until the acquisition of a bovine small intestine. The intestine needs to be expunged of any contents and blown up similarly to the stag bladder. Depending on the collection time frame of these materials, they may need to be stored and preserved safely until the next fall season. At that time, the dried chamomile flower heads are rehydrated with some juice made from fresh chamomile plants, and then stuffed into the small intestine to create a chamomile sausage. It is not for human consumption, so do not eat it. Instead, hang it up and let it air dry for a few days. Then, bury the sausage(s) in the same manner as the yarrow preparation. The following spring, dig up the sausage(s) and collect the flowers and chop up what remains of the intestine, letting it air dry. The flowerheads and the remnants of the organ are ready for use as a compost additive. The chamomile preparation has been noted to increase soil vitality and help ward against plant malformations.

Nettle - *Urtica dioica*

The nettle preparation requires no organs or animal parts. To begin, nettle patches are scythed down at the first sign of flowering and left to wilt for a few hours. A pit will need to be dug in the same way as previously illustrated. It can be scaled up or down in size, depending on the volume of nettles you have. Line the pit with peat moss, and place the nettles in the center. For overall convenience, the nettles can be stuffed into a burlap sack, or something equivalent, and placed into the center of the pit. On top of the nettles place a large board or some pieces of wood. That way, when the nettles start to break down, the wood will compress with it and make harvesting later easier. Surround the sack with the peat moss, then mound up the pit with the excavated earth. Let the nettles remain in the pit an entire year. Then dig them up and repeat the process. The harvested nettles can be stored and used as needed in the compost pile.

Oak Bark - *Quercus* spp.

The oak bark preparation is another very involved process requiring unique materials. It is recommended to harvest the bark from a mature tree, at least thirty years old, towards the end of summer. You will also need a skull from a  livestock animal. Ideally, a cow, but pig, sheep, goat, etc. are all acceptable. The oak bark is crumbled up very fine and placed into the skull at the end of the summer. If health regulations allow, and you have a pond on your property, bury the skull filled with the oak bark in the sedimentary sludge of the pond. If that is not an option, fill a barrel with a generous amount of plant refuse and water, letting it turn into sludge. Place the barrel so that drain gutters flood the container when it rains, causing it to overflow. Then bury the skull inside the sludge of the container. In the spring, retrieve the skull and harvest the oak bark from within. At this time, the preparation can be used in the compost pile or stored as needed. The oak bark preparation aids in regulating excessive growth in plants and helps ward against fungal infections.

Dandelion - *Taraxacum officinale*

The dandelion preparation also makes use of an organ from a cow. In this preparation, the mesentery—a sheath-like tissue that encloses and attaches several of the internal organs to the wall of the abdomen—is used in conjunction with dande-

lion flowers. The first step is to harvest dandelion flowerheads in early spring before their cones are fully open, and dry them as you would for preparing a tea. The mesentery is to be obtained immediately after the cow is slaughtered and given a few days to dry in the sun. In the fall, rehydrate the dandelion flowerheads and the mesentery with a juice made from fresh dandelions. Be sure to properly store the mesentery so it does not spoil or attract bugs or animals if there is a gap between the harvesting of the materials and the fall.

To compile the preparation, the mesentery is cut up into squares anywhere from eight to fifteen inches in size. Then, several handfuls of dandelion flowers are placed on each square and packed up into a dumpling shape tied with a string. These dandelion dumplings are left to air dry for a couple of days. Once they have dried out a little, bury the dumplings in a pit constructed in the same manner as the yarrow preparation. The following spring the dumplings are dug up and are ready for use or to be stored.

Valerian - *Valeriana officinalis*

The valerian preparation is the last of the compost preparations described here and does not require any animal parts. It is purely in liquid form, which differs from the others in this section. Being virtually just a fermentation product, it is more straightforward and easy to produce. The first step is to harvest valerian flowers. Once gathered, they are chopped up and juiced. The juice is then put into a glass fermentation bottle with a tube to allow gases to escape. Store the bottle(s) of valerian juice in a cool dark place for at least six months, letting it fully ferment. The bottle(s) can be sealed off completely after this fermentation process and allowed to continue to mature for several years. This preparation is used to hydrate the compost pile, and it promotes thermophilic activity and warmth as well as attracting earthworms into the pile.

VERMICULTURE

Vermiculture can have several meanings, depending on the context, but basically, it means the cultivation of worms. There are thousands of species of worms, and their taxonomic placement is based on their ecological role and behavior. Three broad classifications of worms are relevant to greenhouse management—endogeic, anecic, and epigeic. Endogeic worms live within the soil, creating lateral burrows while feeding on organic material such as dead plant roots. These species are less well known and generally only surface occasionally during abundant rainfall events. Anecic worms create vertical burrows in the soil, from which they surface as needed to drag food back in. Epigeic worms do not develop tunnels or live deep in the earth, but spend the majority of their life above the surface in the duff layer or within compost itself.

In this section, we will touch briefly on worm species within the greenhouse planter, but the bulk of the focus will be on the epigeic group of worms and their utilization in composting. Worm composting systems are a wonderful addition to a composting paradigm of any size. Due to the generally smaller size of these setups, they can be a primary means for low-volume composting where space is a premium. For example, if your greenhouse is a part of a studio Earthship and the overall square footage is limited, or even for an urban gardening operation. Throughout this section, think of ways that could work for you to weave vermiculture into your greenhouse management routine.

Most retail vermiculture composting setups are tiered tower systems with a spout on the bottom to drain the excess liquid that builds up, called leachate. These worm composting bins are called a variety of things, like worm condominiums and worm factories. Retail worm bins usually run between $50 and $200, without the worms. A potential downside to purchasing a system like this is that it can take some practice to balance the conditions in the bin. When the environment gets too soggy, it can be a bit smelly and attract bugs; if it is too dry, the worms will slow down their activity. A quick web search for worm bins will give you some DIY options. These can be more affordable than retail ones, or more expensive, depending on how elaborate you want to go. By building a custom one, you could avoid the smelly bug-attracting problems that retail ones can sometimes have, and you could cater the design to fit the specifics of your space at the same time.

Worm composting requires some discernment as to what you put in the bin for the worms to eat. The worms are not able to compost all organic scraps. Some things take a very long time and are not ideal, and some foods are irritants, which is counterproductive. Be sure to note what foods the worms cannot compost—like meat, bones, dairy, and very spicy foods.

Outlined here are the mechanics of a standard retail tiered worm bin setup. Designs may vary, but the functioning will be similar. The way the typical worm bin works is simple. The bottommost tier does not change positions and acts as a basin for excess liquid to pool up in, creating leachate that can be drained from the spout and used as fertilizer, diluted 1:10 in clean water. As described in the fertilizer section, using diluted leachate is viable, but the amount of time the leachate has sat in the bottom tier will affect the amount of living biological organisms in it, which are the primary health engendering ingredients. So, using only leachate can be hit or miss in its effectiveness. At any rate, it will not hurt anything to use it. Making tea from the worm castings is an excellent way to ensure the maximum positive effect in the garden.

All the other tiers are designed to be stackable. They are usually square, but sometimes circular in shape, with small holes along the bottom that allow the worms to migrate around and into different sections of the tower. You start with one box on top of the base, and begin depositing compost scraps inside it, along with some shredded paper or straw. The paper or straw acts as a cover material to absorb excess moisture and reduce smells. Then, you have to acquire the right species of worms to place in the bin to begin the digestion process. It is necessary to get composting worms, specifically. The most predominantly available species that will do the job is *Eisenia fetida*, known by many different common names such as red wiggler, redworm, tiger worm, and so on. The earthworm or nightcrawler that you find in your yard lives and grows under entirely different conditions and has different behavioral patterns and a different diet. If you place them in the worm bins, they will struggle and potentially die. So again, be sure to use the right kind of worm for these bins.

Once the first tier begins to get full, you add another tier on top, following the same process of building up the compost material until the top tier is full. Typically, there are three tiers total, so once the second tier is full, add the last section and repeat the process. By this time, the bottom tier of compost should be fully digested and almost entirely worm castings. Take off the top two tiers, giving you access to the first tier, in which you can then harvest the worm castings. Replace the first tier with the second and the second with the third. Then, place what was the first tier at the bottom onto the top, so it becomes the third tier. Once it gets going, you can follow this cycle of harvesting worm castings, monitoring the bin conditions, and rotating the sections as needed, all while producing a valuable and versatile product for your greenhouse.

Utilizing worms within the planter depends on the planter style, management style, or greywater system you have. In some cases, only one type of worm is appropriate in a greenhouse planter system, and in other cases, all three classifications could find a suitable space to live.

Epigeic worms are a good option for a greenhouse that operates with heavy mulching of some kind. Ideally, they would thrive best in a poly-mulching system, because the mulch layer would provide the correct habitat and the worms would re-

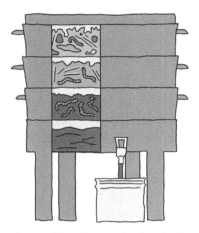

A profile view of a typical tiered worm condo.

ceive a large variety of food sources, containing a more diverse set of nutrition than a mono-mulching system. Any other type of greenhouse operation would be a poor choice for Epigeic worms, because they would not have the right living conditions to grow and propagate. Due to their high fecundity rate and big appetite, epigeic worms are best in their own separate space and in conjunction with your compost paradigm.

Endogeic worms for the garden can be found for sale by a few specialized retailers, but they are hard to come by because it is such a niche market. One reason is simply a lack of awareness and knowledge of worm species. Most people do not know the benefits endogeic worms offer in the garden or how they differ from any other type of worm. So, reduced market demand makes the commercial selling of endogeic worms very rare.

Unbeknownst to most, endogeic worms can play a pivotal role in the transformation of your greenhouse from lackluster to robust and vibrant. Endogeic worms act like a subsurface plow and slow-release fertilization distributor. As they move laterally through the upper soil horizons, they create burrows that aerate the soil and improve water infiltration. They feed on dead and decaying organic material such as plant roots, and their waste is a biologically active source of nutrition.

In a greenhouse setting, this type of worm can be an invaluable asset and is well worth the time and energy to deliberately integrate them into your system. If you observe slow decomposition and consistently poor soil conditions between crops, it is highly advisable to source some endogenic worms for the planter. Adding a handful of them will significantly boost the soil biome's ability to digest and recycle organic material. Except for a soilless or flooded style planter, endogeic worms are an excellent addition to any greenhouse.

For the majority of outdoor gardening or farming operations, these types of worms will appear naturally with no extra effort on the part of the farmer. Unless you amend an interior garden with wild soil, the chances of endogeic worms appearing on their own are slim.

Only a small number of worms is required to colonize a greenhouse setting properly. So, it should not be too expensive if you choose to order from a supplier. As an alternative to buying these types of worms for your greenhouse, they could likely be hand-harvested in your local area after a heavy rainfall. Keep in mind that you would need to be able to identify them correctly.

Anecic worms are widespread and well known. The classic earthworm/nightcrawler is among them. They occasionally surface to pull food, such as leaf litter, down into their vertical burrows in the soil. Their benefits are similar to endogeic worms, which makes them a worthy addition to any greenhouse system that can meet their habitat requirements. Shallow salad bar planters or any soilless planter beds, such as reed beds, will compromise their activity significantly and, in some cases, even kill them due to excessively saturated conditions. So, be sure, wherever you place them in your greenhouse, there is ample soil for these worms to plunge into deeply and have enough freedom to move around. Confined planters may be acceptable, and the worms can adapt to some degree, but their performance will be best if the depth of the planter is more than a couple of feet.

Also, bear in mind, worms from this classification will struggle in a no-mulch greenhouse because they rely on organic material from the surface as their primary food source. In a no-mulch greenhouse, everything gets regular grooming so they will have little to no food, leading to unhealthy worms or an early demise. Alternatively, they thrive in messier systems with lots of mulch, where they have abundant food sources. Anecic worms can easily be harvested in most regions after heavy rains or purchased at a bait shop. Anecic worms can also naturally appear in cured compost piles, as long they have access to the pile directly from the soil.

Greywater Pretreatment With Worms

An experiment that took place in the Earthship greywater planter design was the inclusion of composting worms in the reception cell. This is a small chamber that greywater enters for pretreatment before flooding the rest of the planter cells. Instead of placing a knee-high stocking over the inlet tube in the reception cell to capture and filter out larger particulates like food chunks, the top half of the cell was filled with composting worms and some bedding material for them. The idea behind making the reception cell a worm bin was to allow the worms to digest the food scraps, creating some harvestable worm castings and also flushing the greywater system with worm leachate, making the greywater potentially more nutritious for the plants. While this concept is doable, it requires particular conditions and actions on the part of the user. Much of the kitchen sink drainage contains irritants or less than ideal food sources for the worms, which will significantly inhibit their activity and even, potentially, kill them. Furthermore, with the newer Earthship greywater design, pretreatment via worms becomes altogether obsolete, because the kitchen sink now drains to septic tanks instead of into the greywater system, thereby removing all the nutrition and material the worms would digest. Overall, it would be best to avoid including this aspect into a management system.

LIQUID FERTILIZERS

There are countless home concoctions and recipes that have been brewed up for the garden over the years. We will take a look at several different types to get a feel for the possibilities. The four categories we will review are ready-mix teas, overnight brews, long steep/fermented teas, and intensive brews. The reason for delineating these different types of fertilization is to help clarify and organize your options, as well as aid in effective garden planning. If you know how long things take to brew or how simple or complex the brews are to make, it allows you to anticipate what is the most reasonable choice at any time of year and help you better schedule your garden time. Sometimes, you may need to plan so that fermented teas will be ready at the correct time, or you may be pressed for time during a busy period and need to have a quick shot of nutrition for your garden, in which case ready-mix teas may be the answer. Having a clear understanding of the time investment, resources needed, and complexity of each type of liquid fertilizer will reduce stress and help you pick the best type of liquid fertilizer for any occasion.

For holistic greenhouse management, the bread and butter of the nutrition program stem from the creation of good compost. The best time to add minerals or harder soil amendments is during the building phase of the piles, as I mentioned in the composting section. That is why most extra fertilization comes from liquid sources rather than topdressing. Even with excellent compost, each management style requires some form of supplemental nutrition or support here and there. This section showcases a handful of holistic options that are possible at home with everyday materials. Of course, there are many more options available. Profiling a few types provides a well-rounded foundation. If you visit your local nursery or grow shop, there will be a wide array of commercial fertilizers, supplements, and amendments available. Some will be fully organic, others partially organic, and some chemical or synthetic. As you would imagine, I strongly advise against the use of any chemical or synthetic products because it is counterproductive and not sustainable in running a genuinely holistic greenhouse. In some cases, it may be convenient to purchase some items from your local store, but make sure you take the time to talk with someone there or read the ingredients carefully to ensure you are getting a clean product that you know how and when to apply appropriately.

Each management style will vary in its prioritization of which type of liquid fertilizer to use and the frequency with which to use it. When relevant, the technique and management style will be noted directly in the subsequent sections. It's best to familiarize yourself with these techniques, and once you have a feel for their impact, adjust accordingly for plant needs and seasonal conditions, because most of these recipes have some flexibility. Hanging planters and container plantings will significantly benefit from these techniques as well, because they are nearly entirely dependent on outside inputs for their sustenance.

In general, any fertilizer you buy at the store will have a label with a numeric ratio for the content of macronutrients: N-P-K—nitrogen, phosphorus, potassium. In the store, it will look something like 1-1-1 or 1-5-8. Nitrogen is a critical element in the vegetative stage, when lots of biomass is growing on the plant. Higher nitrogen fertilizers are applied during the period between the first appearance of true leaves and blooming. Phosphorus and potassium aid in flower and fruit formation, and fertilizers containing higher levels of these elements are for the flower and fruiting stage.

It is practical to have a working knowledge of the periodic elements and their function in plant metabolism. I do not place extreme emphasis on it in this book because it becomes less of a critical feature when compost is a central element. A healthy and well-made compost releases and makes available to the plants the correct nutrients, enzymes, and compounds, at the right time, naturally, through the processes of the biological soil organism itself. In the resource section are appropriate links to dive deeper into plant metabolism and diet if you are interested.

As with all other aspects of gardening, learning to balance and use fertilizers in the greenhouse takes time, patience, and experience. It is easy to get discouraged if you over-fertilize and damage the plants or under-fertilize and they struggle. The vast spectrum of information available to someone new to gardening can be intimidating. The main thing is not to give up or be afraid to give new things a try. Just because one season may not pan out the way you might have hoped, and it may seem like forever until you get another chance to correct it, do not let that get you down. Observe and analyze any mistakes and learn from them. Growing your food and taking care of a garden is a worthwhile skill to develop, and no one is perfect at it 100% of the time.

READYMIX TEAS

Molasses

In most homes, you can usually find a dusty, old bottle of molasses in the cupboard, next to all the baking stuff that is rarely used, but this cheap and widely available product is a valuable addition to the health of the greenhouse. A suitable type of molasses is the unsulphured blackstrap variety. All the other types will work, but blackstrap is cheaper and will perform equally as well, if not better, than the other types. Be sure to buy organic, because conventional or feed-grade molasses may contain contaminants inimical to the soil biology.

Molasses is a significant source of minerals, such as iron, calcium, and potassium, which are great to work into your soil. The sugars and carbs in molasses provide a boost to soil organisms, which ultimately leads to improved plant health, as long as administered in moderation. An ideal mixture is a one-quarter cup of molasses per five gallons of water. This combination needs thorough mixing. Warm water will assist in speedy dissolution of the mixture. Put the mixture in a watering can, and then topwater the garden. It is best to wait to incorporate this mix until you have a well-established soil community, and then only use it sparingly as a boost to the biology. Molasses is good to keep in your gardening inventory, because it is not only useful here and there as a quick snack in the form of a soil drench, but it can also be beneficial in aerated compost teas, which we will cover in this section.

Urine

For some people, the use of their urine in the garden may be out of the question. Nevertheless, our bodies manufacture a fantastic fertilizer every day, if we use it correctly. That is, of course, if the source of the urine is healthy itself. If you are sick, detoxing, or have heavy medications in your system, it will affect the urine as a fertilizer, and it's best to avoid it for use on your plants. Urine contains a variety of vitamins and nutrients; the most significant being urea, which is commercially available and a general fertilizer. Urine is best used as a fertilizer during the vegetative growth stage, as it is high in nitrogen due to the urea content. For use as a soil drench, a recommended dilution ratio is 1:10 in water. For a foliar spray, dilute further to a 1:20 ratio. Dilution is essential because raw urine is too concentrated and will burn most plants. Be sure to flush the soil thoroughly with water if you use urine often as a fertilizer. Flushing the soil is crucial because urine contains varying levels of salt, depending on the individual's diet, which can build up in the rhizosphere and cause stress or even kill the plants.

OVERNIGHT BREWS

Worm Casting Tea and Leachate

Not everyone will choose to include a vermiculture setup in their greenhouse system, but if you do, the worm castings and, to a lesser extent, the liquid leachate from the bottom bin, is a free, amazing, and abundant resource. Do not worry, though, if you choose not to have worm bins because worm casting products are for sale at your local shop or online. A little goes a long way, so you will not be breaking the bank if you have to purchase it every so often. Just like with molasses, it can double its functionality by not only being an excellent fertilizer on its own, but also a core ingredient in aerated compost teas.

In the vermiculture section, I pointed out the difference between worm casting tea and leachate. Worm castings are a soil-like by-product created by the worms digesting the organic material. The highest concentration of worm castings is in the bottom bin of a worm composting setup. Leachate is the excess liquid that builds up in the bottommost part of a worm bin that has a spout attached to drain it out. Diluted leachate will not harm the plants as a fertilizer, but its effectiveness will fluctuate, depending on how long it has sat in the bottom of the worm bin. The longer it sits there, the more biological forces die off, which are what stimulates the desired health-giving effects for the plants.

It is, therefore, advisable to create more reliable leachate from harvested worm castings diluted in clean water. Making your tea will guarantee that all the health-bolstering effects take place when you use it. A cup or two of worm castings to five gallons of water is a good ratio. You can either drop the castings directly into the water, in which case you may have to screen out any sediment if you are going to apply it as a spray, or place it in an old cloth or mesh sac to act as a tea bag. Then it is ready to use, as is, immediately after steeping. Either way you choose, the process is simple. Dilute the worm castings in water, let steep overnight, then apply to the plants. If you have a lot of space to cover in the garden, you can further dilute the mixture to extend its usage.

I have not shied away from using the leachate, even though there is lots of conflicting information on this topic. From my personal experience, I have had amazing results, or at least no negative results, from applying some, diluted, in the garden. One such case comes to mind. I had just transplanted some small seedlings out into a planter. A week went by, and they looked like they could use a boost, so I drained some leachate from the worm bin and diluted it 1:10 in a watering can. I then went around and gave all the new seedlings a little drink. In that batch of seedlings was a dinosaur kale. This one plant in particular either loved whatever was in that leachate or was just naturally very robust, because it began to soar past all the other plants. That kale went on to become so enormous that it reached the ceiling, which was about eight feet high. One morning, I had come into check on the greenhouse, and one of the off-shoot branches of this kale had gotten so large and heavy it had broken off and was lying in the planter. Many clones are from this plant and the seeds were saved to continue propagating in the future. This plant may have been a bit of an anomaly, being extraordinarily vigorous, and maybe the leachate did not help it grow that much, but it certainly did not hinder anything.

Eggshell Tea

Eggshells are another common and easily accessible resource that can be put to good use in the garden. Ground up, it can be put into the compost pile as an amendment, but it is equally as good as a soil drench. To make an eggshell brew, take around ten to twenty cleaned and dry eggshells, and pour a gallon of boiling water over them in a bucket. As you can imagine, it is best to use fresh organic farm eggs rather than factory-farmed. Just like any amendment, the healthier and more natural the product, the better its function will be in the garden. Once you have poured the boiling water over the eggshells, let it sit and steep overnight. The following day, strain out the eggshells and the tea is ready for top watering your planters. In a healthy greenhouse system, a reasonable frequency of use is once a week to once a month. Of course, any surplus eggshells can be added to the compost.

Eggshells are rich in calcium, and this is an important element in any plant-based system. Calcium acts as the skeletal structure for building a strong, resilient frame in a plethora of biological organisms. When pest pressure and diseases prevail in your greenhouse system, more often than not, the first link in the chain of deficiencies is a lack of calcium. Many challenges are mitigated by having a system that properly cycles calcium —not just through adding calcium amendments to the soil or compost, but by growing the right types of plants to fix calcium and make it usable by the whole. While the calcium found in eggshells may not directly translate into more calcium in all your plants' biomass, it is still important to continually supply good quality raw materials into the biological organism of either your soil or the compost, so that it can transform, break down, or build up in the way needed.

LONG STEEP/FERMENTED TEAS

Manure Teas

Animal manures, such as cow, pig, chicken, rabbit, etc., are useful as fertilizer in the greenhouse. The process is similar to the previously outlined examples, except the steeping time is longer. The longer you steep manure tea, the stronger the brew becomes. When using animal manures, the waste cannot be too fresh because it will burn the plants. You need to allow time for it to break down and age—a good time frame is around six months. It will be fairly hard and dry when ready, usually crumbling apart when handled. If using chicken manure, it is best to let it age longer than six months, ideally a year, before use as fertilizer. If you have a significant enough amount of manure, another method to speed up the process and safeguard from any potential illness-causing sources is to make a compost pile specifically of manure.

To make the brew, the ratio of water to manure is 5:1. With chicken manure, it is best to dilute it even further, to 10:1. For a five-gallon bucket brew, put a good helping of manure at the bottom of the bucket, then fill it up with water. Mix it thoroughly, then put an old shirt or cheesecloth over the lid of the bucket and tie it down tight with a string or cord. Place the bucket in a warm, shaded area and let it sit for a week to three weeks. You can stir the bucket occasionally if you want, but it is not mandatory. If you are in a real pinch for time, you can use the mixture earlier than a week, but it becomes more potent the longer you let it sit. When it is good and ripe, you can pour some in a watering can and dilute it further to extend its usage. Apply as a topical soil drench.

Ruderal Brew

Ruderal plants are often considered weeds. They are hardy pioneer species that colonize disturbed, mismanaged, or waste areas. Although some people find their presence a constant nuisance, they are packed full of good stuff for the garden, if you know how to make use of them.

To make the brew, pull up or chop down any common weeds like dandelion or bindweed. Next, you need two five-gallon buckets. Take one and drill small holes all around the bottom. This bucket gets placed inside the other bucket and stuffed with all the plants you collected. Pour a big pot of boiling water over the plants, and fill up the buckets the rest of the way with warm water. Cover with a shirt or cheesecloth and tie it off. Let this sit in a warm, shady area for at least a week. Again, the longer you let it sit, the stronger the brew gets. When it starts to smell pungent, you know it is good to go. Take off the lid covering, add some more water if it is sludgy, and give it another stir. Slowly lift the top bucket from the bottom, allowing the tea to drain into the bottom bucket it was stacked in. You can use a stick and some more water to squeeze out and flush all the juice from the plant material, which is probably a big pile of mush by now. Once done, you can chuck the leftover mush onto the compost pile. Your ruderal tea brew is ready to use and can be diluted in a watering can to top-water with, or put into a sprayer to apply to leaves.

If your batch was fully fermented, it can be bottled and stored for later use for up to six months. The main downside to this is the smell. It is best applied in the early morning, when you will be out of the house most of the day.

INTENSIVE BREWS

Actively Aerated Compost Tea

Aerated compost tea can be a powerful liquid life force for your garden. The technique combines compost, water, and food sources with lots of air to create an ideal breeding ground for healthy aerobic organisms. The result is a dynamic living brew that can transform or elevate your plant and soil health. The way it works is simple—you use something like compost, worm castings, garden soil, forest soil, etc., as an inoculant/starter for the biological community you want to grow, and then you provide the right food and all the right conditions for a massive population explosion. When applied to the soil, it goes to work.

There are tons of different recipes, depending on the type of soil conditions you are looking to facilitate. There are manual methods of brewing, as opposed to automated alternatives using machines and pumps. In this section, we will cover the more classic, low-tech, manual way of brewing.

In the resource section, there are links to explore the diverse and extensive world of aerated compost teas. Lots of information and courses are available, involving all the specifics, intricacies, and complexities of brewing these teas. These courses cover how to make the perfect compost to use in the tea and also precisely what foods will feed the specific beneficial organisms you want to grow, whether it be bacteria, fungi, protozoa, nematode, and so on. They also explain all the functions various soil entities provide. Time spent studying resources or taking classes can give you great insight into soil biology as a whole. So, if you are new to these concepts, it may be a worthy investment.

Whenever feasible, I attempt to steer away from automation or reliance on machines, opting for as low-tech as possible solutions or practices. That is why I am illustrating the stick in a bucket method and not any new, sophisticated compost tea brewer that is for sale. There is nothing wrong, however, with the use of mechanized options and, given certain circumstances, they make the most sensible and appropriate choice.

For the manual method, you need the following items: a stick (long enough to comfortably reach the bottom of the bucket and be held with two hands for stirring); a vessel for the brew, in this case a clean five-gallon bucket works perfectly; a pound or two of cured compost; some molasses; cheesecloth; a handful of oats; one ounce of humic acid; one ounce of water soluble seaweed; and clean water. One other optional component is a backpack sprayer if you plan on using the tea as a foliar spray.

The recipe presented here can be scaled up or down depending on vessel size. For example, you could also use a fifty-five-gallon drum as long as you can still effectively stir the water. It is also essential to be aware of the temperature. Since you are working with living organisms, their activity is best around 70-75 degrees Fahrenheit or warmer temperatures. Just as with compost piles, if it is too cold or too hot, it will inhibit the process.

Once you have gathered all the materials, fill the bucket with water and tie up a handful of oats in the cheesecloth like a tea bag, and let it steep in the water. Swish the bag around and let it steep for ten minutes or so, then add at least a pound of your chosen compost. Remove the oat tea bag and mix in your molasses, humic acid, and seaweed. Then, aerate the mixture actively. With this aeration method, you create a deep vortex with the stick. Start slowly, stirring either clockwise or counterclockwise, close to the edge of the bucket, in big circles. Once the water starts swirling, you can begin to speed up the rotations, making the water swirl faster and faster. Once you have enough momentum, start tightening the circles toward the center of the bucket while increasing the speed. The goal is to stir fast enough to cause a vortex to form that reaches to the bottom of the bucket. When you reach the point where the vortex has formed, pull the stick out and let it continue on its own. Making a vigorous vortex allows the mixture to become imbued with air and all the surface tension from the move-ment will keep pulling air into the mixture for ten to twenty minutes, depending on how much energy went into the mix. Set a timer for fifteen minutes and, when it goes off, repeat the pro-cess, stirring in the opposite direction this time.

The longer you can aerate the brew in this way, every fif-teen minutes or so, the better. It allows more time for aerobic colonies to form and expand. If you attempt to let it sit over-night, be careful, because if the brew starts to smell fermented, you will have to start over. When I do a big batch, I try to start early in the morning and make applying the tea my last task of the day before I clean up. That way, I can ensure ample time for the brew to mature and not run the risk of losing the batch. It will still be beneficial for your garden if you apply a shorter brew time mixture, but the longer, the better. If you choose to apply the compost tea as a foliar spray, you will need to use the cheesecloth to strain the liquid into the backpack sprayer. If you are not using a sprayer, you can go ahead and apply it as a soil drench.

Aerated compost tea works wonders for establishing new planters, as it instantly installs a thriving biological network into the soil, which can help overcome many barriers and give your system a big head start. These teas are also wonderful to apply intermittently, as a basic upkeep fertilizer in the garden and to help balance healthy soil populations. Some people use aerated compost teas exclusively as their primary fertilization source. This may be something to consider for your greenhouse. At any rate, including this technique in a holistic greenhouse regime can aid in consistently supporting overall vitality and quickly become part of your core toolkit as a greenhouse man-ager.

Biodynamic Spray Preparations

This section will cover horn manure, horn silica, and horsetail spray preparations. If you have read the biodynamic compost section, then you know that the methods to compile these end products are very rigorous and in-depth. I can attest that the results, if done correctly, can be worth all the time and energy. I have seen firsthand the efficacy of some of these preparations, because I have volunteered several times at a local biodynamic farm.

On one occasion, it was time to apply the cow horn manure preparation. We were broadforking the garden rows while the mixture was being brewed and, once it was done, the backpack sprayer was loaded up with the preparation and sprayed out on the soil. It was subtle, but to my surprise, it seemed to take an almost immediate effect. The soil that was broadforked was clumpy, hard, and dry, and with just a little misting from the backpack sprayer, the soil texture changed before my eyes. I picked some up, and it felt like it was softening and loosening into a more comfortable structure. I was finishing broadforking the last garden row as the preparation was sprayed on the portion that was left for me to finish. In this section, the soil was significantly more responsive and easier to work with than the previous rows. I was a bit confounded that such a little bit of water could have that effect, but as I thought about it, it reminded me of the initial action that homeopathic remedies can cause when first administered. I then recalled from the agriculture lectures by Dr. Steiner that, indeed, some of these preparations were made to work in a homeopathic-esqe manner (See lecture 5 of the agriculture course, paragraphs 5 and 6 for one such reference).

I have reflected on that experience many times, and I feel that the power of these concoctions starts to make more sense when you use them firsthand. Outright, some of the preparations sound outrageous, but perhaps as time goes on and their efficacy continues to be verified, these preparations will seem more sensible to our modern minds. These methods may not be for everyone, but it is still a worthy pursuit to obtain a cursory knowledge of these practices even, if you never plan on implementing them in your system.

The Horn Preps

As one might imagine, the horn preparations require cow horns from a freshly slaughtered cow. The horns may be reused several times for a few years, as long as they remain in good condition, but with the silica preparation, the horns may only be used once and then composted. In each method, the horns get stuffed with material and buried in the ground, in the same manner as described in the compost preparation section, to mature for a season and become imbued with active forces.

In the case of the manure preparation, the horns are stuffed with cow manure, and with the silica preparation the horns are packed with a finely powdered quartz made into a paste with rainwater. The manure preparation is buried at the end of fall and dug up in the spring, and the silica preparation is buried in the spring and dug up in the fall. These preparations can be seen as polar to each other in the timing of their composition, application, and their scope of action. The manure preparation acts as a soil stimulant and works chiefly within the rhizosphere below ground. The silica preparation works above ground upon the aerial parts of the plants, and its impact is primarily on the stabilization of growth and metabolic forces. Both of these ultimately get utilized as a spray for soil or crops, but applied at different times. Generally, the manure preparation will be used at the start of spring and again in the fall to boost the soil life activity or assist in seed germination. The silica preparation is for use at varying intervals depending on the plant's growth stage.

It is best used after true leaves form to equalize the growth forces, by either promoting more growth in a slow-growing plant or helping to slow and calm down excessive growth in a very vigorous plant. The silica preparation is usable as needed until blooming, flowering, and fruiting starts. Then, cease any further application.

The preparation of these into a form usable for spray application is very similar to manually aerated compost teas. Dump a portion of the contents of the horns into a barrel or vat, then aerate it by creating a vortex with a stick or pole of some kind. Be sure that the manure and the silica preparation are not combined, but done individually at separate times. The proportions will vary, depending on the area that needs to be covered and the preparation you are using. Once the contents of the horn are in the water, it is then actively aerated via the method described in the aerated compost tea section, but with no breaks for at least an hour. So, in this method, there is a constant vortex the entire time, which can be very labor intensive for the individual performing the mixing, and it may be advisable to do quick swaps on rotation with another person or two to reduce the strain. After the aeration is complete, the mixture should be applied the same day, as letting it sit overnight or trying to store it will compromise its efficacy. The finished mixture is then added to a backpack sprayer and applied as needed.

Horsetail

The horsetail preparation does not exclusively belong to biodynamics, but since it is in the main lineup of preparations, it is fitting to place it here. This preparation is unique in that it has multiple recipes, depending on where you source it, that are all useful and valid. The horsetail preparation is usable as a ready-mix tea, an overnight brew, or a fermented tea, and they are all effective. This brewing flexibility is a wonderful asset,

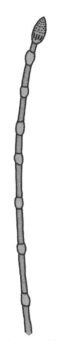

provided you have access to a patch of this plant to harvest. Not everyone will, but it is a fairly cosmopolitan plant, usually found near streams or riverbanks.

Horsetail—*Equisetum arvense*—is a very old and unique plant. The bulk of plants found in our world today are angiosperms that reproduce through pollinated flowers that create seeds. Horsetail is a vascular plant whose reproduction is from spores instead of seeds, making it uncommon in this regard. It bioaccumulates silica, which is a valuable mineral for plant health in many ways. Silica can increase cuticle strength in plant leaves and stems, which acts to bolster immunity and tolerance to both pests and extreme environmental conditions. Silica also provides a regulating action on detrimental fungal activity in the soil, helping the plants to remain healthy and balanced. I have found a foliar horsetail tea to be especially helpful for greenhouse plants in New Mexico's dry summer climate. Even in a greenhouse full of lush biomass, it is challenging to avoid lower humidity levels and desiccating winds that stress plants not climatized to these conditions. A foliar spray may not be as ideal for a more humid climate, and a soil drench is likely much more advantageous to curb excessive fungal activity in the rhizosphere. Regardless of climate, if you have access to this valuable plant, it can prove very versatile and useful in your greenhouse management regime.

A biodynamic mode of preparation for horsetail fits naturally under the ready-mix tea section, as it only takes an hour and, then, it is ready for use. The procedure is as follows: harvest what horsetail is available and then dry it as you would a tea. Take about half a pound of plant material in two gallons of water and simmer for an hour. Strain, if needed, and then dilute 1:10 in clean water. Apply as necessary.

All the other recipes for horsetail teas are fairly similar, and it is straightforward to make any modifications that suit your time frame. A more extended version of a horsetail preparation is done by pouring boiling water over the horsetail in a bucket and letting it sit overnight. Then, strain and keep to the same dilution ratio as above before applying. Another method is to pour a soup pot full of boiling water over some horsetail in a bucket, and then fill it the rest of the way with warm water. Cover with cheesecloth and tie it snugly to the top of the bucket. Let it stand at least a week or more to ferment, which will depend on the weather. Once it has broken down enough and smells pretty funky, strain, dilute, and apply as needed. Add the sludgy contents to the compost pile to further extend its usage.

MULTISPECIES COVER CROPPING

Many will be familiar with the terms "cover crop" or "green manure," but this practice takes that concept a big step further. In most cases of cover cropping in agriculture, a single species of plant is grown in between cash crop rotations or intercropped between planting rows. A widespread example of a well-known cover crop is buckwheat—*Fagopyrum esculentum*. What differs between these methods is what the name describes. Instead of using a single species within a cropping system, fifteen or more plants can be grown in unison that act powerfully upon the soil and local environment, producing numerous effects that positively interplay.

Amazingly, there is a group of progressive large-scale farmers who have advanced these cover crop blends and rotations to an incredibly precise, organized, and sophisticated system. These farmers have dialed in many specifics, like proper seeding rates per acre, to ratios and percentages of seeds per blend. Cover crop blends have been designed to handle a whole host of needs and challenges, such as grazing mixes for livestock, soil compaction relief blends, weed suppression mixes, soil builder blends, and so on. All of these are fine-tuned for the season, the climate, the soil, and the other crops grown on the land. Researching and following their protocols can produce astounding results on any scale of growing operation. See the resource section for links to this material. Multi-species cover cropping is the core mechanic that enables a poly-mulch greenhouse management style to operate effectively. It can be incorporated, to a lesser extent, in the other management styles, but is fundamental to a poly-mulching system.

The benefits of practicing an intensive cover cropping system in the greenhouse are many. Stacking rotations of various blends of cover crops will give you the most diverse yields of all the management styles. Well-built and designed blends improve soil structure, fertility, organic matter levels, nutrient cycling, moisture retention, and stimulate productive and healthy biological activity. With a well-constructed cover blend, the greenhouse manager reduces dependence on outside sources of fertilization, because the crops themselves are the fertilizers and produce what is needed organically. All these features also help to mitigate pest pressure through biodiversity as well as improved systemic health.

Working with a smaller footprint allows you more flexibility to control and manage termination or harvest times. Any of the cover crops that produce a yield of some kind are harvestable by the greenhouse manager, providing a unique array of products throughout the year. This aspect is an added benefit that usually is skipped over, or not feasible, on large-scale operations because of the risk of the plants reseeding or the farmer not being able to properly terminate the cover crops.

Farmers utilizing this type of cover cropping system have a small window, when the plants are flowering, to roll or chop the cover crops down to terminate them. This is because when the plants are in this stage, they are expending the majority of their resources towards flowering and producing seeds. This metabolic activity in the plant leaves little reserve in the root systems, making them susceptible to being fully killed off when chopped or rolled down onto the soil. The timing of termination is critical in bigger systems, because if the cover crops have enough vigor to regrow after an attempted termination, it can have negative impacts on the output and quality of the next cash crop.

Furthermore, if mature seed heads are allowed to form in more substantial systems that rely heavily on machinery, it can cause havoc in the fields, and the cover crops can become a reseeding weed problem that consumes lots of time and energy. These are huge concerns in bigger farming systems. But, within a home greenhouse, if the termination is not perfect and a few plants resprout, or some mature seed heads fall on the soil and germinate, it does not have a devastating effect. The plants that persist through an attempted termination in the greenhouse, either from the root itself or from seed, can just be incorporated into the next round of cover crops and terminated at an appropriate time.

Smaller home greenhouse settings also allow for more control over canopy structure and grow space optimization. Doing multi-species cover crops on this scale enables you to trellis, train, and prune your crops as they grow for optimal spacing and growth. Micro-managing like this is not an economical option when operating a more extensive system, because manually setting up bean poles and stakes and pruning leaves to balance sunlight for all the plants would require either incredibly specialized machinery or many working hours. Being able to manipulate the cover crop blend as it grows enables maximum biomass production for all the plants in your blend. For example, if your beans sprouted quickly and spread leaves out laterally in a dense fashion, some of your lower-lying crops in the blend, such as turnips or radishes, could have their growth staunched or even completely blocked due to lack of sunlight. Instead, the beans can easily be trellised or staked so that growth is encouraged vertically, allowing the slower-growing or low-lying crops a substantial opportunity to reach maturity. Trellising also creates the best use of the growing space in the greenhouse by taking advantage of all the room from floor to ceiling, as well as capturing as much solar gain as possible.

A last major perk to working on a smaller scale is it opens up more varieties of plants to incorporate into your blends, because on a larger scale many seeds would not be economical to use. So, many cover crop blends popular on an industrial scale can be emulated, but instead of following the mix exactly as prescribed, some plants can be substituted or added for more exciting, productive, or interesting crops for your greenhouse.

There are a few benefits, though, that have reduced efficacy in the greenhouse as opposed to an exterior garden. Within the greenhouse, attracting pollinator or predator insects is less viable or useful because it is designed to be a barrier, preventing wild forces from entering. Nevertheless, pests find their way in, so it can be helpful to get an occasional beneficial insect or two into the space when the weather permits. Soil compaction is most likely not going to be a huge factor, unless it is in an in-ground planter that is already on poor soil, or if less than ideal soil was installed into the planters initially. In this case, it would be wise to run a couple of seasons of soil-building cover blends to improve the planter conditions before switching to another style of management. Frost or colder temperatures terminate certain cover crop blends. Since the greenhouse prevents near-freezing temperatures from occurring, the only viable means of terminating winter-kill cover crop blends is to manually chop them down at the base during flowering. Although, winter-kill blends are a great way to start working with this type of system in an outdoor garden.

Cover crop species have separate categories, based on their morphology and function in the environment. Different organizations provide more or fewer categories and, in some cases, certain plants overlap into multiple groups. We will elaborate on the categories that are most suited to the greenhouse, rather than large-scale agriculture. We will look at three main groups and, to a lesser degree, a miscellaneous fourth group. These categories are nitrogen fixers, tubers, grasses, and multi-function. Aside from their main categories, cover crops can be further subdivided by their seasonal growing requirements and ease of management, making it convenient to construct a blend that works well for a particular season and meet whatever needs are at hand.

Nitrogen fixers belong to the Fabaceae family, which includes beans, clovers, vetches, and peas. The nitrogen fixer in a cover crop blend becomes the engine for biomass generation that fuels and sustains the rest of the plants to grow to optimal size. They leave behind available nitrogen for the next batch of plants to utilize as well. Plants from this family are widely used as green manures to replenish nitrogen in the soil after running a cash crop. They form a relationship with nitrogen-fixing bacteria that nodulate on their root systems and absorb nitrogen gas from the air, making it accessible in the rhizosphere. It is critical when incorporating plants from this family into a blend to inoculate the seeds with the correct bacteria that form nodules on the roots. Many seed companies offer the inoculant at affordable prices, and it may be at your local nursery or farm store. There are links in the resource section to online suppliers. Nitrogen fixers take advantage of the free and abundant nitrogen in the air, allowing the greenhouse manager to significantly reduce dependency on outside sources of fertilization. In many cases, bean pods can be harvested and stored for later use.

Tubers, the second group, can mine nutrients, causing them to swell up in size and provide many great functions within a cover crop blend. There are many suitable varieties of radishes or turnips that can fulfill this role. The large, bulky root systems that form break up soil compaction and improve soil structure, aeration, and water infiltration. Tubers also act as a nutrient storage tank, due to all the nutrient mining in the soil, which in turn becomes a slow-release fertilizer, if left to decompose in the soil. If harvested, they make another excellent edible yield from your greenhouse. So either way, it is a positive outcome.

Grasses, the third group, belong to the Poaceae family. Good examples of cover crops from this family are barley, triticale, millet, and rye. Grasses fix calcium, which is key to the health of subsequent crops grown in the soil. They produce large amounts of biomass, which turns into nutrient-rich mulch. They aid in water infiltration and improve soil structure. They are also effective at scavenging excess nutrients in the soil, helping to maintain overall balanced ratios in the rhizosphere. If left to go to seed, small batches of grain can be harvested for use in culinary pursuits.

The last group, multi-function, contains plants that have

reduced effectiveness in the greenhouse or are just used to a lesser extent. Some of the functions they provide are bio-accumulation of minerals via deep root systems, soil fumigation from secondary metabolites, beneficial insect attraction or deterrence from volatile essential compounds, early pest indication through incompatibility with the soil biome, and weed suppression via competitive leaf canopy structure and vigorous root growth. A couple of examples of dynamic accumulators are chicory and dandelion. Most brassicas or mustards will perform some degree of soil fumigation, which helps balance the rhizosphere and inhibit unhealthy growth. Buckwheat is effective for pollinator insects, and parsley family plants help attract beneficial predatory insects. Early pest indication plants can vary widely, as described in the plant archetype and functions section. An excellent plant for weed suppression is hairy vetch. It can become a weed, though, in the greenhouse because of its hardiness and difficulty to terminate. Therefore, it is not recommended for use in this style of greenhouse management. Plants performing these functions may be suitable to incorporate occasionally in a poly-mulch system, simply because they provide a good edible product that works well with a particular blend.

The balanced construction of a cover crop blend takes into account the varied abilities that plants from each of these categories offer. As you can see, combining them can create a dynamic synergy that radically changes the soil and greenhouse conditions for the better. Beans can fuel the other plants' growth. Tubers can aerate the soil and provide slow release fertilization. Grasses can build up the foundational elements in the soil and create a robust framework for subsequent plants. Minerals can be pulled up from deeper soil horizons to higher areas. And, cover blends can offer pest deterrence and pollinator attraction. There are many other effects, all at the same time, in a single blend. For every situation, a specialized composition can be made from anywhere from two to twenty plants, or even more if the circumstances call for it. Weaving a cover cropping system into the greenhouse can drastically change the management experience, as well as be very fun and rewarding.

The best practice when getting started with multi-species cover cropping is to first consult with a business that has plenty of experience on the topic and can help you design the right blend for your particular needs. They will be able to provide the correct inoculant for the beans, as well as tell you the proper seeding rates for your system and what to expect in terms of plant termination times. Once you get a feel for the process, you can branch out and start experimenting with construction of your blends, catered to any goals you may have. It can be as easy as going to the local health food store and building your cover crop blend from what is available. I have done a successful cover blend from pearl barley, flaxseed, buckwheat, pinto beans, soybean, mung bean, and sunflower—which can generally all be found, very inexpensive, in the bulk section of the grocery store. Of course, for best results, you would have to get the right bean inoculant.

Let's say you have a cover crop blend prepared, you know the right seeding rate for your greenhouse, and you have the right inoculant for your nitrogen fixers. Remember to either wash your hands promptly after handling the seeds or use gloves. The first step in planting out this blend is to create a slurry in a bowl of water with a spoonful of molasses and the inoculant. Once the slurry is ready, after thorough mixing, fold in the beans if they are separate from the other seeds, or mix in all the seeds if they are together. Stir well to ensure proper adhesion of the inoculant to the seeds. Now scoop out portions of the cover blend from the inoculant mixture and scatter the seeds onto the surface of the planter soil. It is normal for pockets and patches to form in the planter, where one particular plant species tends to pop up more than others, but it is crucial during the seed broadcasting time to make sure there is an even distribution of seed types across the soil surface.

The even dispersion of seeds is necessary because all the

plants need to intermingle for maximum benefits. Do do not neatly organize each seed type into rows or try to plant them out strategically. This technique is designed to be messy and organic, and as long as you have the correct seeding rate and you evenly distribute the seeds, the spacing and sizing will balance itself out. After broadcasting the seeds onto the surface, work them into the soil. This can be done by hand or with a rake or hoe if the greenhouse space is large enough. The seeds need to be pushed down into the soil at least an inch or so, and covered again with topsoil. Take note beforehand of any special requirements certain seeds in your blend may have. Some may need to be left on the surface for germination; others may have a specific depth to be in the soil to properly germinate. If this is the case, seed them out by themselves after this step to give these plants the best germination rate.

For the first few weeks after the blend is seeded out, the planter needs to have the equivalent of at least one inch of rainfall per week. Watering is ideally done in increments over several days, because it is important not to let the soil dry out during germination and seedling establishment. As the blend grows towards the flowering stage, you need to continue to monitor soil moisture levels and water as needed. Any plants that can need to be be trellised or trained. Trellising promotes the best light penetration in the planter and makes the most use of the active growing space. Depending on the conditions of your greenhouse, it is wise to apply an occasional misting with clean water over the plants to wash off any dust or debris on the leaves and simulate natural environmental patterns. There is no need to worry about fertilizing the plants as they grow, because the beans, peas, or vetches should be providing the fuel the system needs to mature.

Before the plants reach the flowering stage, you need to decide if you are going to chop the whole blend down for use as a mulch all at once, or allow some or all of the plants to reach full maturity for harvesting. If you plan to terminate the blend as a whole, once all the plants enter the flowering stage, cut them down at the base with some large pruners or a scythe, if the space permits. As you chop, lay the organic material evenly on the topsoil as a mulch. If you want to harvest only a few plants and chop the rest, follow the same process, but you will have to be more delicate when cutting the other plants down to not infringe on the ones you intend to harvest. Lastly, if you plan on allowing all the plants to reach full maturity for harvesting purposes, wait until you have collected what you could from the plants and then chop them all down, laying them as mulch onto the topsoil.

There are many possibilities for incorporating this style of management into your greenhouse system. Since it is relatively uncommon, it provides the opportunity to be creative. For example, it could be practiced indefinitely as the main cropping routine to obtain a broad spectrum of yields. It could be used for a few seasons to build up the soil and then switch to a perennial-dominated greenhouse. After a series of heavy feeding plant rotations, it could be used to rebuild the soil, or it could even be used in small sections of an established planter to boost diversity. It will be up to you to determine if exploring this method is suitable for your management style.

CHAPTER V

PEST AND DISEASE

Even if a greenhouse is managed flawlessly, it is an inevitability to contend at some point with pests and disease. Like it says in the introduction, this challenge will inevitably emerge, and no greenhouse is a hands-off utopia. Many factors influence the total health of the greenhouse—the source of seeds, environmental conditions, substrate quality, pruning practices, and general hygiene. All these and more play a role. This chapter will address the many elements that affect the health of your greenhouse system from a broad integrative point of view.

ECOLOGICAL SUCCESSION AND THE GREENHOUSE

Ecological succession is a process observed in landscapes over time. It is the progressive development from simpler to more and more complex biological communities in an ecosystem. After a major climatic event that devastates the landscape in some way, this process is visible. The most common example is the stages of a forest after a wildfire. In the year following the fire, a forest is left quite barren, with maybe only a few plants emerging during optimal growing times. From the second year on, slowly, a larger variety of plants begin to colonize the landscape. After the period of little to no growth, mainly annual flowering plants and grasses start to grow, then some smaller perennials in the subsequent years. During this early stage of succession, the soil biome is rebuilding, and the landscape begins to be able to support a more extensive array of animals. As time continues, shrubs and smaller trees germinate, and what was mainly a grassland ecosystem for some years starts its metamorphosis into a mixed forest again. This organic progression leads to a climax period in which the forest is at its peak form, hosting its maximum level of diversity on all layers.

Ultimately, this cycle is destined to repeat, and as the climax stage wanes in vigor and approaches its end, a fire is a normal function to reset the pattern of ecological succession. Seeing this entire process, of course, takes much longer to witness fully than what is possible in a human lifespan, and often it does not happen in such a direct and clear way due to human intervention. But, understanding this inherent process in nature can help in formulating a harmonious perspective for your greenhouse system.

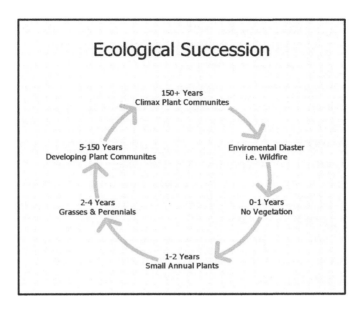

Ecological succession is a relentless driving force in the organic world. When engaging in any agricultural activity, this underlying natural process is inescapable. There is nothing in our toolkit to fundamentally alter its mechanics; we can only work within its boundaries. From a farming perspective, as biological systems become more complex and host a broader range of organisms, we see an increased level of autonomy. In this way, we can see ecological succession as a spectrum in agriculture.

Each style of farming will fall somewhere on the scale of this successionary cycle, whether it be monoculture, greenhouse polyculture, food foresting, no-till, or wild foraging. When farming with a particular style, we constantly intervene in the successionary cycle to maintain the appropriate stage for the method we choose. The more biologically complex and integrated the farming system is, the more autonomous it is from the need for external inputs and the farmer. In turn, the simpler and less biologically complex the farming operation, the more dependent it is on external inputs and the farmer.

For example, to run a mono-culture based system, tremendous amounts of energy and resources are required to suppress the upward successional drive of nature. Forced simplicity in ecological systems over prolonged periods is counter to the patterns of nature, and therefore, it becomes increasingly difficult to manage the longer its operation continues. Monoculture systems attempt to keep the soil and the plant systems at a very early stage of succession. The intensely maintained simplicity would place this on one end of the spectrum. On the other end, would be a practice that relies entirely on foraging in the woods, like mushroom hunting. The forest is a biologically complex polyculture, and there is very little, if any, energy and resources used by the farmer to obtain a yield.

The style of greenhouse management presented here would teeter somewhere in the middle of these extremes. A "managed greenhouse poly-culture" is the best label for it. Operating a home greenhouse in this way offers a plethora of benefits to the manager. There is a reduced workload, increased health, more diverse yields, a beautiful aesthetic, and much more. See the following image to understand the workload and input levels better. This image represents general expectations, and any type of farming could be adapted or pushed more to one end of the spectrum or the other, depending on the individual farmer.

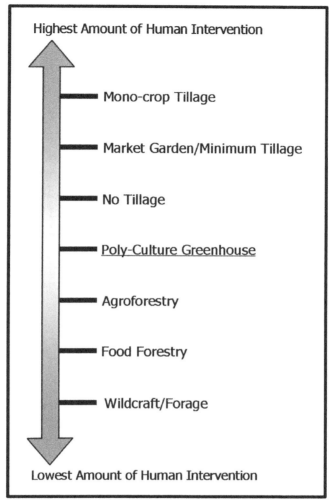

A chart showing where Earthship greenhouse management falls on the spectrum of ecological succession and farming methods.

HOLISTIC PARADIGM
FUNDAMENTALS

A prevailing attitude, in far more than just agriculture, is an "identify a problem and obliterate it" mentality. This only works in the sense that it temporarily removes something from the equation, but does not deal with underlying causation. In extreme cases, this may be the best viable mode to handle an overwhelming event, but as a primary means of interaction, it perpetuates any challenges you are facing. Reacting in such a way is only a Band-aid to buy time in dire situations, and should be seen and used as such. If operating your greenhouse in a manner outlined in this book, aggressive measures should become more and more rare.

One example where extreme action in the greenhouse would be necessary is if somehow the interior greywater system got inoculated with E. coli, and became a breeding ground for disease. In that case, a total overhaul would be in order. This is highly unlikely if proper procedures are followed, and especially so if a greenhouse is operated holistically, as we will elaborate. At nearly every nursery store insecticidal soaps or even stronger poisons can be purchased to kill unwanted pests. There are also countless home remedies, and in some cases, it may be warranted to employ these. However, the aim of this book is to take a step back from the common modality and offer a more integrated and gentler approach.

The foundation for holistic greenhouse management is all about balance and emulating nature. For many people, the world of agriculture and gardening can be opaque and full of complicated scientific terms. This seemingly impenetrable exterior can cause many to believe that only well-educated soil scientists or people who have a natural green thumb are able to be successful with their gardening endeavors. As awe-inspiring and mystical as this would be, it is not the case.

Everyone can become a good steward of their landscape, and it does not require a doctorate in soil biology or a divine talent. Nature may be mysterious and complex, but there is order, reason, and meaning to its patterns and functions—not total random chaos. It is all connected. Traditional teaching has trained many people to believe that when interacting with the organic world, in the form of gardening or farming, all of the natural laws that apply universally in every ecosystem do not apply to the garden, and whatever they attempt is expensive, challenging, and overly complicated. Working under this framework can certainly be discouraging, but in this section we will try and dispel some myths about holistic approaches, as well as dismantle the current hegemonic beliefs ardently propagated by the agricultural authorities.

Every greenhouse structure continues to remain subject to the hierarchy and laws of the natural world, regardless of how well sealed off it is from its external environment. The influences of the exterior surroundings can be modified and altered to some degree, but the mechanics of health and disease will persist in every case. We will build from a few observations found in nature, and translate them to inform our perspective on the management of health and disease in the greenhouse.

The first and principle observation is that nature produces no waste. There are only by-products and resources, and they are the same. The varied forms and organisms in every ecosystem interplay to consistently transform, metamorphose, and recycle all the material and contents found there. What is one being's waste is another's fuel. This complex and dynamic interaction reveals a subtle layer of symbiosis. While destruction, eradication, illness, and death are all part of this cycle, sophisticated and mature reciprocity is deeply embedded in the natural order. Organisms and organic forces behave as though they understand the mutual interdependence required for the harmonious operation of the whole. This survivalistic impulse and its effects preserve the integrity and wellness of the entire system.

The principle of "produce no waste" can can be further distilled into reciprocal survivalistic homeostasis. In this definition, even disease, sickness, and death perform necessary functions to balance the development of any organic system. The tiniest or the largest living entity within this domain provides a functional niche that aids in the chorus of homeostasis in some way. As everything in the ecosystem is part of a living jigsaw puzzle, there are stratums and jurisdictions for all the organisms to complete their roles. Since the driving impetus is towards preservation of the whole and, to some degree, harmony, organisms inherently act on behalf of the whole as a form of biofiltration. This biofiltration is the result of the transformations, metamorphoses, and recycling action that the whole host of natural forces constantly perform. It is more than just a filtration process; it is a perpetual bio-rectification that purges and purifies life forms that are unfit to progress, and pressures them to become stronger. Each species or form is uniquely equipped to fill a particular niche, which either safeguards or amplifies total systemic health.

This niche function is what is happening when plants become afflicted with pests or disease, and it is not haphazard. There is structure, meaning, and significance to everything that arises within the greenhouse. Whatever suboptimal influence that reveals itself in the greenhouse is acting as an indicator of what requires filtration from the food chain, and why. When disease conditions emerge, it is simply an alarm that there is something out of balance or a deficiency that is causing compromised activity in the health of your system. In a holistic worldview disease is simply biofeedback. In a conventional agricultural worldview, this biofeedback is responded to with extreme force, demolishing the alarm in hopes that the alarm itself was the issue, and once destroyed, everything will conform to the goals and the will of the farmer. Time and experience have made it abundantly clear that this type of practice becomes increasingly more challenging and expensive, while producing a less than ideal result.

Operating more healthily and constructively when disease conditions show up is to attempt to ennoble the surrounding environment, thereby improving the health of the afflicted entity, and not instantly destroy the messengers. The terms "pest" and "disease" are illusions that act as labels, based on our experience of them. This is not to say it is not painful or challenging, or to devalue the reality of the effects. Nature works systematically, and the appearance of pests and disease is both meaningful and organized. There is a tiered pattern we can observe. The progressive process of biological decline begins with bacterial issues, then fungal, viral, and, lastly, pests and parasites.

Understanding this pattern and process of nature is very eye-opening, because it sheds light on the seemingly chaotic and unpredictable forces of nature, making them insightful instead of confusing. When the greenhouse manager realizes that by the time aphids or whitefly or any other pests arrive on the scene, there have already been several deficient or missing links in the chain of health that need to be brought back into alignment. From this perspective, the pests are a wake-up call to look deeper into your system and all around you instead of outright waging war against some insects just doing their job. When a biological system, no matter how big or small, has influences pushing it down the path of compromised health, it is not the fault of the manifestation or pathology, but of a variety of forces lining up in such a way as to preserve the natural order of life.

Using this information to contend with challenges in the greenhouse can be counter-intuitive to what is familiar, but, ultimately, it is empowering, once we are acquainted with it. This requires astute observation and discernment. Sometimes, things may need to be added to fill a gap that is causing a deficiency; other times, removing or reducing certain components will be necessary because they are creating an oversaturation, imbalance, or are not compatible with the current stage of the broader biological community. The holistic process includes the entire system in its assessment of issues, and starts by promoting balance in all components before taking any form of aggressive action.

NUTRITION AND HEALTH

Balance is key in any biological system. Conventional modes of agriculture, in the realm of nutrition and growth, stem from a reductionist worldview that places hyper-emphasis on particular fundamental elements, like nitrogen, phosphorus, and potassium. This emphasis creates a specific understanding of certain biological interactions, which have enormous value and importance, but can miss the mark when attempting to formulate a holistic gardening modality that respects the full complexity of natural systems. Suffice it to say there are boundaries to our natural science, and while much has been achieved, there is more going on with the living activity of the earth and its inhabitants than we fully comprehend, as of now.

Conventional wisdom on mineral nutrition and fertilization can be misleading. Healthy proportions of both macro and micronutrients need to be present for all the niches and functions of a robust biome to perform optimally. There are a few key elements that play a critical role in the overall health and wellness of life in your greenhouse. Surrounding these elements is a shroud of misinformation, misunderstandings, and possibly even willful neglect.

Introduced in the prior section was the concept of the natural order of disease in the organic world. This progressive process reflects degrees of health, and as the plants get sicker, they become afflicted with different types of pests or diseases. To reiterate this pattern, it starts with bacterial issues, then moves to fungal problems, then viral and finally pests/parasites. Each of these stages is an indicator of the severity of the condition and health level of the plant(s). As the scale slides away from bacterial issues towards the appearance of pests/parasites, each type of disease or imbalance can be seen as a step down.

How does the pattern of the natural order of disease, as out-lined in the previous section, inform or have any bearing on plant nutrition? From the vantage point of fertilization and mineral amendments, this progressive decline in health tethers to sequential nutrient deficiencies—a concept formed through the careful study of plant deficiencies in conjunction with the emergence of disease.

What is outlined here is simple and straightforward, but outside the mainstream canon of agricultural methodology. Testing these conclusions for yourself could save you many painstaking failures and frustrations, and provide you with an essential bit of knowledge to diagnose and remedy numerous afflictions, without sophisticated or complex instruments. The "Ecological Succession and the Greenhouse" section outlines the progressive stages of biological communities developing into more and more complex systems. Observing the early successional stages reveals a key component—primarily, grasses emerge early on and initiate the improvement of soil conditions through the recycling of their organic material. Why do grasses develop so early on? What role do they fill? Why does the climax species not emerge first, since they take so long to grow? Because, the soil and environmental conditions require priming and building up of biology to properly support the trajectory of their growth cycle. Grasses fix calcium in their biomass and, when digested by the soil, produce a myriad of critical life-engendering effects used in biological systems at every stage of life. Calcium fixation early on in the successional cycle sets the ecosystem up for success, because it is a fundamental building block of life.

Calcium is the most misunderstood and misused element in the agricultural world. It is the foundation on which everything else builds. It is in cell tissues and membranes, working as nature's way of armoring the living entity. It is the intermediary for which other nutrients interface to transform, metabolize, or release their contents. Calcium is the predominant factor in determining total biomass. It also performs vital detoxification functions, organically regulating the plant's immune system and making it incompatible with disease-engendering forces, insoluble forms of fertilizer, and so on. For truly healthy soil and plants, the biological organ of your greenhouse must cycle the appropriate organic form of calcium. Without it as the backbone of your garden, the greenhouse is destined to perpetually struggle with various problems, and perhaps even lead to system collapse.

Misunderstanding and misappropriation surround another nutrient of fundamental importance—phosphorus. This element does much more than support flower and fruit production. It facilitates healthy nutrient transport and assimilation within the plant, as well as aids in sugar production from photosynthesis. It also has a primary role in the creation of genetic material, which is invaluable for the health and wellness of future plants.

So, if you combine the main functions of both of these elements, you can see how they lay the foundation for all metabolic activity in plants. If improper levels of calcium and phosphorus are not found cycling in a biological system, in the vast majority of cases, it can be observed that the declining health pattern of bacterial, fungal, viral, and pests will initiate in the system. The manifestation of multitudes of pests on a whole host of different plants stems from insufficient levels of calcium and phosphorous. Compared to conventional wisdom on agricultural nutrition, this perspective is a far cry from anything you would hear from many authorities. As stated above, while these two elements are fundamental to the greenhouse or any biological system, all macro and micronutrients need to be present and in balance for success as well. This bit of foundational knowledge gives the greenhouse manager a clear starting point to begin diagnosing and contending with any emerging challenges.

There are many sources available that can provide the mineral nutrition your greenhouse needs. Bone meal is an excellent base to start with, because it contains good quantities of both calcium and phosphorus. Be sure to remember, in this style of greenhouse management, all harder amendments are best added to the composting process, and then applied to the greenhouse through the vehicle of cured compost. Allowing the amendments to go through the composting action accelerates the breakdown process into plant-soluble forms, and better integrates them into the biological community.

One could say that holistic practices attempt to work from the inside out, and conventional models from the outside in. Again, the main message here is a change in worldview from attacking symptoms to understanding why certain symptoms exist. This way of thinking requires more in-depth investigation and patience on the part of the manager, but ultimately establishes the health of the greenhouse more authentically.

PESTS

In the conventional model of dealing with pests, there is often very little thought given to what conditions precipitate the arrival of one type of pest over another. For the most part, what caused their appearance is considered irrelevant, and all that matters is what products or practices are required to get rid of them. The information provided here is mainly an attempt to dismantle the natural reaction instilled in us to panic, reach for some insecticide of varying lethality, and then automatically start waging war against the insect. Reacting in this way only serves to further dissociate you from what your greenhouse is telling you and obscure the originating causes of any detrimental forces, thereby compounding the issue.

When operating from a holistic standpoint, the reason why one pest appears over another is valuable because pests are a side effect of a deeper problem, and not the problem itself. By the time pests arrive, there have already been several conditions that have initiated a decline in health. Understanding the environmental stresses allows you to properly delineate and divide one issue from another, thereby getting closer to the source of the problem, and to work to keep them from arising as naturally as possible. This is an inclusive model in which you are an extension of the living organism of the greenhouse. It is then your job to participate in the changing conditions, throughout the seasons, and do your best to emulate functions and patterns that nature performs instead of waging war against unwanted influences, such as bugs. Instead, the bugs can become your ally in health, giving you the clues you need to balance the whole and achieve your greenhouse goals.

Working within a greenhouse affords the ability to control and make modifications to the environment to a much greater extent than outdoor operations that are beholden to the sway of the weather. In a greenhouse, it is idealistic to aim for a totally pest-free zone. As seasons pass, some plants mature, others die and find a replacement, and new nutritional or environmental inputs add to the system. Therefore, the greenhouse is always in some degree of flux and development. With this constant motion, the presence of certain pests in moderation is a much more realistic expectation because there are many microbiomes that are adapting, expanding, or growing. Understanding that "pests" will never be fully extinguished from the greenhouse is simply adhering to a worldview that is in accord with a more holistic reflection of natural processes. Instead of working against these forces, they are co-opted to assist you as a feedback system that allows you to better serve and integrate with your greenhouse. By either reducing or adding to the level of biological complexity in certain areas, the greenhouse manager is constantly intervening in this dynamic living process in an attempt to maintain a balanced and managed ecosystem. Regardless of how robust a soil biome is, it would be unnatural for no pests to exist, because, at every stage of ecosystemic development, many insects are present. It is just a matter of balanced populations. The various insect populations that take up residence in the greenhouse are there because they are biofilters, integral to the positive successional pattern taking part in your gardening system.

When these insects emerge in a manner counter to your goals, it is time to take a step back and discern what is happening. Check the afflicted plant. Is it entirely covered, or just a section? Is it a massive outbreak affecting the whole greenhouse, or localized in a particular region of the planter? Is it a single species of insects, or are there two or three? It is important not to act rashly, but to gather data first.

In some cases, the emergence of a single species on an isolated plant could be alerting you to the fact that your soil biome is maturing well, and that particular plant is no longer suitable to associate with the current stage of the biological community in the soil. An isolated plant no longer compatible with a developing soil biome is a wonderful alarm, which requires no aggression or hasty action. Instead, the plant and its localized area can be monitored and then replaced with a plant appropriate for the current level of succession.

From my observations, I have compiled a list of environmental greenhouse conditions that either promote or deter certain pests from making an appearance. Understanding this aids in diagnosis and beginning a remedial process to restore the habitat to a more balanced and wholesome state. There are many species that a greenhouse manager may run into, and only a handful of common pests is presented in this section. This will provide a starting point for understanding how to observe events or challenges in your greenhouse and respond constructively.

Whitefly - *Trialeurodes vaporariorum*

As their common name implies, whiteflies are tiny, white flying insects—much smaller than a pinky fingernail, usually about two millimeters

A closeup of a single whitefly on a leaf.

long and three millimeters wide. They often appear on the underside of leaves and suck sap from the plant's biomass. In large numbers, they can cause significant damage to the afflicted plants and even lead to death. In addition to the damage to plants, they are also conduits for amplifying a variety of fungal issues. Whiteflies produce a sticky, sugary substance called honeydew, which is often unsightly on the plants and can damage them and bring in other insects that are attracted to the honeydew.

When whiteflies arrive in the greenhouse, two particular environmental indications can work in unison or separately that make their appearance more likely over other species. First is excessive stillness or lack of movement in the aerial parts of the plants—a deficiency of airflow or physical contact. On the majority of occasions when I have discovered whiteflies, they were in a location that did not catch any natural breezes from the skylights, operable windows, or doors. The other condition also has to do with lack of movement, but in the soil. When compacted soil conditions staunch the healthy formation and expansion of plant roots, this repression causes a weakening stagnation in the plant's system that mirrors the lack of airflow in the aerial parts of the plant. One or both of these conditions, coupled with sequential nutrient deficiencies in the greenhouse system, is likely to usher in a flush of whiteflies as the first form of insect biofiltration.

Most people will have at least one or two areas in the greenhouse that do not receive ample airflow. In this case, it is recommended that the manager makes it a point, during pruning or cleanup sessions, to manually provide some airflow to the plants in the buffered zones. Adding manual aeration can be as simple as using a sheet of cardboard as a fan for a few minutes here and there or, if solar power allows, plugging in a fan for a while during the day. This is effective because it fulfills a natural requirement of the plant, in a fashion that emulates nature. Instead of waiting until the bugs arrive in an area of the greenhouse already struggling because of a lack of natural forces, you can be preemptive and modify those conditions before they become too extreme. As far as remedying soil compaction, the holistic and organic methods outlined in this book take time, but provide an ideal protocol to improve the rhizosphere.

Aphids - *Aphis* spp.

The type of aphids you will most likely see in the greenhouse are small, often portly looking insects that come in a

A small colony of female aphids.

variety of colors. They quickly form dense colonies on afflicted plants, because they have a very high reproduction rate. Aphids can decimate crops and act as vectors for other plant viruses and molds. As with most of the insects profiled here, they also secrete honeydew, which can tarnish the plants and entice other insects into the greenhouse.

The appearance of aphids stems from unfulfilled metabolic potential. This could come from a shock that signals the plant to do more than is sustainable, or from poor plant placement, which could staunch what would otherwise be strong growth. Either of these causes suppression of metabolic forces and creates a sort of oversaturation in the plant that is appetizing to aphids. This suppressed activity, coupled with sequential nutrient deficiencies, is a precursor to an aphid infestation.

For example, let us look at a plant that had good germination and ideal nutritional sources as it grew to the flowering stage. It may have taken some time for the plant to reach this stage, during which the amount of solar gain it received every day slowly became less and less. Let us add into the equation, perhaps, a disproportionate increase in fertilizer added to boost the plant in the flowering stage. Reduced sunlight at the peak flowering time, coupled with a shock of fertilizer, causes the plant to want to grow beyond what the environment will sustain. The result is stress and imbalance. So, what would have been a reasonably healthy plant (its only shortcomings being maybe a reduced volume of fruit or flowers) comes dangerously close to starting the chain of events calling forth aphids to digest it, if the imbalances do not receive attention.

Another scenario, isolating just the effect of poor plant placement, is of a young plant that has good vigor, but is in too shady a part of the planter. Without sufficient sunlight to match its growth potential, the plant will become taxed and, if left too long, it is highly likely that aphids will appear. The best practice to ward off aphids is good plant placement in the greenhouse, keeping in mind how the sunlight may change throughout the plant's lifespan, and exercising moderation in fertilization application.

Scale Subfamilies—Coccidae & Pseudococcidae

The scale family of insects spans a broad range of shapes, sizes, and many genuses. All scale family insects share classification under the superfamily Coccoidea. General observations covered here on the conditions that spawn certain types of scale are for species from two of the most common subfamilies that appear in the greenhouse. Coccidae is the subfamily of soft scale, and Pseudococcidae is the subfamily of mealybugs. Both of these insects suck the sap from plants and, just like most other pests, can be vectors for other diseases as well as form a relationship to other insects, which can compound problems and multiply populations.

Green Scale—*Coccus viridis*

At some point, it is highly likely you will contend with this species or one of its close relatives in the greenhouse. Soft scales, in general, can be associated with imbalances generated from overstimulation and excess coming from something in the environment, whether it be human-caused or natural. The overstimulation

A patch of green scale with a few ants harvesting honeydew secrections.

can come from a variety of sources, such as a high volume of foot traffic that continually sends vibrations into the planter, stressing the root system, too much noise in close proximity to the plants, or too much physical contact or handling. It can also come from an over-ventilated greenhouse, stressing the plants with too much wind. In addition to overstimulation, any excessive movements or repositioning of potted plants can act as a stressor for scale to appear. The best remedy is to be aware of any of these potential problems and try to dial back or insulate the plants from overbearing influences in the greenhouse.

Hibiscus Mealybug—*Maconellicoccus hirsutus*

A single mealybug feeding on a stem node.

Mealybugs will form small groups on plants and, once they start feeding heavily, white cottony masses surround them, obscuring their bodies underneath. Aside from the very common hibiscus mealybug, some other species that look and behave similarly might appear, such as *Paracoccus marginatus* and *Planococcus citri*. Whatever the species, if they fall under the mealybug family, the conditions that initiate their appearance will be about the same as with the green scale and its close relatives—excessive stimulation or too much movement. The main differentiating aspect is that mealybugs tend to appear in shadier areas whenever possible, avoiding the hottest and sunniest areas of the greenhouse.

The same applies as with the soft scale in regards to trying to deter mealybugs from manifesting in the greenhouse. Keep any excessive stimulus to a minimum and try to shield the plants from overwhelming external forces. Another measure I highly recommend is introducing the mealybug predator insect known as "mealybug destroyer"—*Cryptolaemus montrouzieri*. Biocontrols can be useful in a variety of cases, and part of a holistic regime, but I do not often recommend them. Mealybug destroyer is one exception, because I purchased them once to combat a mealybug infestation and they did a fine job. Moreover, they actually took up residence in the greenhouse and became a part of the system, producing many generations and helping to stabilize mealybug populations. So, the recommendation for mealybug destroyers comes from a place of permanent integration into the greenhouse, rather than a quick one-time fix, which is much more in keeping with a holistic methodology.

Spider Mites—Tetranychidae

There are many species of spider mites under the Tetranychidae family of mites. When they appear in the greenhouse, you will see a fine webbing starting to cover a leaf or a cluster of leaves. Upon closer inspection, you will see tiny, usually red, insects crawling all around. As they establish themselves, they damage the leaves, creating spots and blotching. If left alone, they can expand to cover the entire plant and even kill it.

High magnification close up of a spider mite.

In the greenhouse, spider mites are more prone to appear than other insects, when plants experience abnormalities or too many differences in environmental inputs. This means that temperature, airflow, or sunlight levels are impacting the plant in a manner that causes confusion and destabilization, because it is out of balance in some way. For example, let us look at a tall tomato plant that is trellised up from the floor to the ceiling. The growth and vigor of the plant may initially have been strong and healthy, but once it reaches its maximum size, it could be in danger of becoming afflicted with spider mites. Because of its height and size, it spans a set of artificial microclimates, created vertically in the greenhouse, that it would not normally experience in nature. These artificial microclimates affect the top, middle, bottom, and root zones differently. Each area of the plant will have very different temperatures throughout the day, as well as nonuniform fluctuations in temperature between day and night.

The uppermost parts of the plant will be subject to any pooling of heat that is trying to escape through skylights and, depending on the style of the greenhouse, they may also have the most intense direct solar gain. In the nighttime, the top of the plant will experience the biggest change in microclimate, compared to the rest of the plant. Since the Earthship uses thermal mass to store temperatures and the upper and the middle parts of the plant shade the lower portions, the base and root zones constantly stay cool, with little to no fluctuations in temperature between day and night. The middle section is generally the most balanced in terms of natural patterns, but since the top and bottom vary so much, having a section that is ideal only contributes to stressing the plant further.

If you compare these different conditions all taking place with a single plant, it is easy to see how abnormal it is and why it would be taxing the plant. Essentially, any inputs that cause extremes in conditions from one part of the plant to another section can contribute to the presence of spider mites.

Another condition that could precipitate spider mites on a larger plant is heavy airflow on one side and little to none on the other. So, one side is being stressed from too much air, and the other side is experiencing stress because of a lack of airflow. An example like this would be more common with the use of mechanical components, like fans and vents.

The best way to deter spider mites from your greenhouse

is through proper plant placement. Try to anticipate the maximum size and shape of each plant and avoid introducing one in an area that could cause too much chaos and stress. If you suspect a particular area of the planter will be an issue for a certain plant, and it is unavoidable, try to pair a partner plant with it, or practice diligent pruning to help buffer any potentially negative extremes.

BEST PRACTICES AND USEFUL TOOLS

One of the most critical aspects of your greenhouse management will be how you use your tools and maintain them. Good pruning practices are highly advantageous. A properly executed, clean cut will stimulate the plant and even help ward off disease. The core tools every greenhouse manager needs are at least one of each of the following: two-hand lopper, garden shear/hand pruner, smaller bypass pruner, sharpening stone, small hand trowel, spray bottle or backpack sprayer, and a jeweler's loupe. These constitute the bare-bones essentials, and many additional gadgets and tools can be acquired to assist in a variety of ways. If you are serious about your horticultural endeavors, do not skimp on the essentials. When it comes to these hand tools, you get what you pay for, and it is well worth your money to buy a quality product.

For a two-hand lopper, expect to pay between $50 and $100. For garden shears for pruning, expect to pay between $40 and $80. Smaller bypass pruners for fine trimming and snipping will be between $20 and $60. I always opt for scissor-based models over spring-loaded ones for fine trimming, because I find I have more control when making precise cuts.

You will also want to invest in a good sharpening stone and, if you are not already familiar with how to sharpen a blade, take some time to practice on an old worn-out tool to get the hang of it. Working with dull blades in the greenhouse can be one of the most discouraging and frustrating things for a gardener, not to mention how badly it can damage plants. There is no better feeling than being able to work smoothly throughout your greenhouse, making perfect satisfying cuts as you go.

If you take good care of your tools, it will contribute greatly to an enjoyable working experience. Regular maintenance of your blade-based tools is an important task to weave into your time in the greenhouse. Aside from keeping a sharp edge, any moving parts like springs or gears should be periodically lubricated with some 3-In-One oil to prevent sticking and preserve the metal. This can be done quickly by applying a drop of oil, topically, on the moving parts before use. As you go about your duties in the greenhouse, the oil will naturally work its way in and provide good coverage.

On occasion, these tools can use a full dismantle to provide a deeper clean in any of the nooks and crannies that slowly get residue buildup or start to get sticky. After each session in the greenhouse, or when working with a particularly pest-infested or diseased plant, it is wise to sterilize your tools. Do this by soaking the blades in isopropyl alcohol, and then wiping them down with a clean rag, or by doing a few passes with a lighter over the blades. I always keep an extra bottle of isopropyl alcohol in my gardening storage area, so that my tools do not go too long without a cleaning. Being attentive to this task is one of the best defenses for stopping the spread of pests and disease.

A jeweler's loupe becomes invaluable to the greenhouse manager for early pest detection. So many of the pests that emerge in the greenhouse start tiny and in very small numbers, easily missed by the naked eye when casually moving through. It is always a good idea to throw a loupe into your pocket any time you plan to do a little work in the greenhouse. Inevitably, you may suspect some insects somewhere and have every intention of running to grab the jewelers loupe to check it out before you're done, but you will get sidetracked and forget to run back and check. I cannot tell you how many times this has happened to me, only to find out later there were some white-flies or something else emerging where I suspected.

Small magnifying glasses also work very well. Many horticultural companies make specialized tools for this purpose with a variety of bells and whistles. Some products will go up to 60x magnification, but I have found 10x–30x is more than sufficient for most early pest detection. Nowadays, nearly everyone has a phone with a camera in it with them all day, every day. There are clip-on macro lenses made for smart devices that can work just as effectively as a jeweler's loupe, and may be far more convenient than remembering to carry around a loupe. A nice bonus with using a clip-on macro lens is that you can take a photo of whatever insect you find for more detailed research and analysis later on.

A secondary lot of tools that can aid the greenhouse manager include soft-bristle paint brushes, twine or twist-ties, small stakes, and a brix refractometer. Paint brushes help increase fruit yield. Since only a small number of pollinating insects will make their way into the greenhouse, their function can easily be filled in with the use of paint brushes. Have a clean brush dedicated to each flowering plant that will bear fruit. As the flowers open, take the brush and gently collect some pollen from the flower and deposit it onto the next flower, and so on. In the case of plants with both male and female flowers, collect the pollen from the male flowers and deposit it onto the pistil of the female flower. Paint brushes also come in handy for plants that have airborne pollination potential, like tomatoes. Just use a light back-and-forth motion over the flowerheads, moving from flower cluster to flower cluster. This technique will greatly improve the total volume of tomatoes, as well as a wide variety of other plants.

Since the greenhouse has a limited amount of space, and plants need to be trellised and trained to conform best, twine, jute, or twist-ties are always in demand. Some type of cordage is coupled with small stakes, whether they be wood, bamboo, metal, or plastic. You will find yourself often needing to make different configurations of cord and stakes to get the best structure for the plants and maximize the growing space.

Another useful tool to have in the arsenal is a Brix refractometer. These are commonly used to check the health of plants and produce. A simple $20 model will do the job, so there is no need to spend a fortune on a very high-end version. A refractometer looks like a small telescope with a clear plate on the end. Samples of juice or pulp are placed on the plate and held up to the light. When you look through the refractometer, there is a numeric scale that indicates the sugar quantity and, in turn, mineralization level. The higher the rating, the healthier the plant. This tool can help confirm the quality of any product you are generating, as well as clue you into any potential issues that may appear in your plants before they physically manifest pathologically.

If you are unfamiliar with working with many plants at once, I recommend picking up a biodynamic planting calendar. It provides a great framework for beginners and advanced alike to discern what days are best for certain activities. If you feel completely lost about when to do what, having this book can help ground you and get you on the right track. Over time, natural rhythms form between you and your plants, and it becomes second nature to pick good days to water or prune or what have you. Once you start to feel more comfortable and gain more hands-on experience, the calendar could still be a reference when needed for larger projects. For example, if you need to have a big transplanting day, where several larger plants are being taken out and replaced at the same time, it is wise to check the calendar beforehand and pick the next day that is most suitable for digging and rooting activities. Even if you are not into the more esoteric origins of the material, the essential information you need to plan your gardening regime is plain and straightforward.

Every greenhouse and manager is unique. So, when it comes to what works best, it is a matter of personal preference in catering your tools and daily rhythms to your needs. The links provided in the helpful links section at the end of this book are the tools I use. I highly recommend these products and, in general, they are a good starting point if you are planning to get yourself equipped for some work in the greenhouse.

SEEDS AND SEED SAVING

Seeds are alive. They are integral to the development and progression of the entire planet, and as such, integral to running a holistic greenhouse. The quality of your seeds will dictate the health of your plants. As your greenhouse matures, the more you grow your favorite plants and harvest their seeds for propagation, the more attuned the future generations of your plants become to your particular greenhouse and climate. Ultimately, where you source your seeds, how you save them, store them, and reuse them all play into the health and wellness of your greenhouse.

Ideally, you start by sourcing your seeds or plants from a reputable heirloom, non-GMO, organic supplier. The seed source may be a neighbor, local nursery, or online. There are many solid seed companies out there, and in the helpful links section, I share some of the companies I trust. A great place for sourcing seeds is to check locally and see if your area has any seed swaps. Seed swaps have different names, but occur when people in your community meet up and trade seeds. Attending one of these can be an avenue for obtaining native and locally adapted seeds for your climate, as well as meeting new people. Of course, the greenhouse allows wider flexibility in plant selection than just local and native plants, and having a mix of different seeds in your seed bank never hurts. It can also be invaluable to meet experienced gardeners in your area who can impart some wisdom to you if you are new.

Once you have quality seeds, there are a few things to consider—such as how, where, and in what you will store them, if they have any special germination requirements, and, once you grow them out, if they have any special means of harvesting. Everyone will develop their own system for seed storage, and as your bank grows, the system will need to evolve too. When you are starting, it is good to have a baseline structure in place that will expand easily as your seed collection grows. Having a cursory knowledge of seed mechanics and what is acceptable or not for storage options goes a long way in maintaining a healthy and viable seed bank.

When storing your seeds, organization and labeling is key. The more rigorous your labeling, the easier it is to manage your bank as it grows. For most people, the common name of the plant will suffice, but if you know the genus and species, it is a good idea to add that to the seed's container as well. It can become confusing, sometimes, with just common names, as they can differ from region to region, and even different plants can share the same common name. Adding the date of harvest to the container is helpful, because you can then track seed quality and performance from season to season. Maybe you get an amazing group of seeds one year, or you end up with some duds another year. It is nice to be able to recall any conditions in the greenhouse that may have affected the quality of the seeds, and either try to repeat them, or avoid them if the result was less than ideal. Also, ten years down the road, when you open your seed bank, you will likely not remember what year those kale seeds are from. The date can clue you into if the seeds will be viable or not. Good record keeping will help in keeping your seed bank up to date and free up space, instead of holding on to seeds that probably are not worth it anymore.

When storing seeds, maintain cooler temperatures, no sunlight, and no moisture. Many seed companies and gardeners successfully store their seeds in a freezer. Freezing seeds, in many cases, can increase their viability by many years. Freezers are wonderful. I have nothing against them, but relying on electricity and machines that can be prone to failure is something I choose not to do, unless I have to. In the context of Earthship-based principles, I opt to store my seeds in the cooling tube of the home as a more low-tech and low-risk means of storage that works very well. A basement, root cellar, or a cool back room are all acceptable options.

The containers in which you store your seeds are also important. Seeds need to breathe and exchange gases. They are not just inert objects that magically grow into plants; they are living entities. In my opinion, if you have the space, money, and dedication, the best option for storage is unglazed clay pots with lids. These most closely mirror how and where seeds are naturally in the wild. Clay pots have mass, so they aid in keeping a stable temperature, and also block out any sunlight. Finding suitable clay pots for seed storage can be a challenge because there are not many, if any, companies that specialize in making them for this purpose. Often, you can find earthen cookware that is very expensive and may be too large for a small greenhouse seed bank application. If you are able to make your pottery, that would be the easiest route, as you could make a variety of sizes affordably.

Second to unglazed clay pots are resealable paper packets. These are ubiquitous, cheap, and work very well. The packets allow the seeds to breathe and can also keep out light, depending on the color and material. Glass containers also work well, but it is extra important to keep them out of the sunlight. Avoiding plastic is smart if you are serious about your seed bank, but in some cases, it may not be able to be avoided, so do not shy away from using plastic if you need to.

When you buy seeds or trade them with friends, always check to see if there are any particular things you need to know to cultivate and harvest them successfully. If you run into issues with germination, before you toss the whole batch, it is wise to take time and research the specifics of that plant to see if you are missing some key element to success. Seeds are in a sort of low-powered sleep mode, only using a tiny bit of resources from within to stay in a dormancy state. Many seeds have what are called dormancy locks, which need to be triggered for the seed to germinate. Examples are cold stratification, where the seeds need to experience a certain amount of cold temperatures before germinating, and some require scarring on the outer shell to break the armoring and allow water to enter to start the germination process. Awareness of seed dormancy locks is something to bear in mind as your seed bank grows. If you end up having any issues with germination via more basic methods, such as overnight soaking and then planting in potting mix, or direct seeding, be sure to look up information on the plant and see if there is a dormancy lock that needs to be broken to have proper germination.

Certain seeds require specific harvesting techniques. As there is a multitude of plant shapes and sizes, so too do seeds come in all shapes and sizes. Since the focus of this style of greenhouse management is not on producing a single large crop at a time, it is generally not overwhelming to harvest plants by hand, without the use of complicated machinery. Understanding some fundamentals surrounding seed typology is sufficient.

Some seeds, like beets, amaranth, and other cereal grains, require an easy three-step process when it is time to harvest. You start by using some pruners or a hand sickle to cut the seed heads from the stalk or base of the plant, and place them in a brown paper bag. If any leafy parts of the plant are still green, you need to let them dry so that it all becomes crispy. Once all the organic material surrounding the seed head is dry, thoroughly crunch up the bag with your hands, making sure it is closed so nothing falls out. Next, take a baking tray and pour out portions of the bag onto the tray. Gently sift the tray to level any big clumps, and then blow on the tray in a parallel fashion. What happens is all the dried organic material blows off of the tray, because it is lighter than the seeds. You should then have a tray of seeds that is debris-free and ready to be packaged and stored. Rinse and repeat with all the harvestable seeds from the plant.

The second example is seeds that have a pulp coating, like tomatoes and melons. In this case, you need a fine mesh hand strainer, water to rinse the seeds, and a paper towel to dry them. Once you cut the fruit open, scoop the pulp with the seeds in it and place some into the hand strainer. Give them a good rinse and pick out any larger chunks that will not fit through the strainer. Next, place the seeds on the paper towel and pat them dry. Repeat as necessary to clean and dry all the seeds. After you have them all set out on paper towels, let them dry for a day on the counter, away from direct sunlight. The next day, they are ready to be packed, labeled, and stored in the seed bank.

Another type of plant, like an apricot, has its seed encased inside a shell or a pit. To properly harvest this type of seed, you must crack the shell and obtain the seed from within. If you have a nutcracker handy, it makes the job easy and quick. If not, you can place the seed on a hard surface that will not be damaged by some gentle tapping with a hammer. Turn the shell on its side, so when you tap on it, you are hitting the seam that connects the two sides of the shell. Pinch the sides of the shell and hold it with one seam firmly on the hard surface. Using the other hand, take the hammer and tap on the seam that is facing you until it cracks open, revealing the seed inside. Repeat for all the pits you have, and the seeds are ready to be packed and stored. You can do this when you go to plant the seeds, but it is recommended to do it before you store them, because the pits are bulky and take up a lot of space in your seed bank. So, unless you have a massive storage area, it is a good idea to do this at the time you harvest the fruits.

Seeds are amazing pieces of advanced technology. They are like little treasures of living history that participate in the future. Each one is a tiny, unique genetic planet all its own. Observing seeds, from my point of view, is one of the best reflections of the macrocosm and the microcosm combined, because it requires sensitivity to the mystery of life itself. Watching plants grow from seed is like witnessing a planet exploding into the broader universe, revealing its inner nature to a brave new world. As my seed bank grows, I feel like the steward and guardian of a million miniature galaxies. For me, collecting seeds is one of the most fun, exciting, and rewarding aspects of greenhouse management.

CHAPTER VI

A YEAR OF GREENHOUSE MANAGEMENT

Working within the greenhouse should be a joy. For many, it may be a time to clear one's head and meditate, or it could even be a time to catch up on podcasts. No matter how you cut it, the time spent in the greenhouse should be special and enjoyable. Ideally, it becomes less and less of a chore and more and more of something to look forward too. Everyone has different aspirations for their garden, and life often dictates how much time is practical to devote to the greenhouse. This chapter outlines all the fundamental duties and responsibilities that go into each management style throughout the course of a year. If any terms or concepts used are unclear, refer back to the appropriate section for a more detailed explanation. Upon conclusion, take the time to reflect on the subtleties between management styles and discern which method may be the best fit for you and your lifestyle. I wish you all the best in your gardening endeavors and may all your tomato plants be massive.

NO MULCH GREENHOUSE

A no-mulch greenhouse is all about starting strong and keeping it clean. This type of greenhouse is best first established with quality soil. The other two management styles are able to improve soil conditions much more rapidly than this method, because no-mulch relies primarily on fertilization sources outside of its system, whereas more fertilization is generated and retained in the other styles. Starting with a sub-par soil will create an uphill battle for a no-mulch manager, and could lead to early outbreaks of pests and disease. So, it is a worthwhile investment to give your garden a good baseline of amended soil from a local nursery or another reliable source.

Once you have gone through the design process and researched your plant guilds, microclimates, zones, and any other pertinent factors relevant to your greenhouse, it is time to plant out the guilds into their designated spots. The time you do this can vary significantly, depending on your circumstances. Since the greenhouse only loosely mirrors the four seasons, do not hesitate to begin to establish plants into your system any time of year. Be aware of spacing and consider all the information gleaned from the designing process. At this time, you could also weave hanging planters into the space. There will inevitably be some unused space at this time and for the first few years. While the guild systems are maturing is a great time to squeeze out some extra production from your yearly cycle.

Let us say that you began your initial establishment of the greenhouse system in the spring. During this time, you will need to be conscious of balancing ventilation and airflow requirements. The longer days promote more growth and maintain higher ambient temperatures. Only a moderate amount of ventilation during the peak of the day will be necessary in most cases. Cracking a door for a half hour to let a breeze in, or popping the skylights slightly, should be sufficient in early spring. The duration will increase incrementally as summer approaches, and then decrease with the onset of fall into winter.

As your system matures every subsequent spring, you will need to take a few things into account. As early as you can, transplant out any seedlings from the late winter months that are ready to go into the planter. At this time do a few early pest-detections sweeps, using your jeweler's loupe, coupled with some pruning of leaves that are more than 50% damaged or have begun decaying. If some of your perennial plants have started to have a growth surge, check the quality of the new shoots for shape and healthy coloring. Now is a good time to increase the frequency of any soil-drench-based fertilization. Good options for this are an overnight worm castings tea or a small batch of aerated compost tea. Either one of these will provide an extra boost of support for the newer seedlings just transplanted as well as for the older perennial plants getting ready to produce more biomass.

Intermittently, throughout the spring, check your local weather forecast and pick a sunny and hot day to give the aerial parts of your plants a good misting or spray with a hose. Your plants will welcome this, and it will help to shed off the stuffiness of the winter season when they get little to no hose downs. You could pair the spray-down days with top watering, because a no-mulch system dries out quickly compared to the other management styles. Remember to always check the topsoil before you top water. Sometimes it may look dried out at first glance, but once you scratch a half inch or so down, it is evenly moist. It is important to not over water, because waterlogged conditions will easily kill your plants. When watering at any time of year, always take into account your microclimates and judge accordingly. Some pockets of the planter will need more water and others less. If you have a very shady zone, only occasionally provide a splash of water, or, if you have an area that always dries out, be sure to compensate with extra watering. Over time this will become second nature as you make your rounds.

Routinely, throughout every season in a no-mulch greenhouse, you will need to do pruning and deadheading, collecting the organic material and depositing it onto the compost. The most optimal method of composting in this style of management is the turn bin setup. If you adhere to this protocol, the end of spring will be a good time to apply a layer of finished compost. More than likely, the batch of compost that will be ready is the pile that was close to a cooling or curing phase before winter, but then went dormant because of freezing temperatures. As the moderate temperatures of spring return, that pile will finish composting and be ready for application by the middle to the end of spring. Once the pile is sifted and well cured, load up your wheelbarrow and spread one to two inches uniformly onto the topsoil. If you operate a no-mulch greenhouse, be sure to review the composting section because it is critical to generate high-quality compost on site, as it becomes the primary source for nutrition in your system.

When it comes to hanging planters, spring is one of two times of year to do a full reset and start fresh. The late winter is an important time to get a large bulk of seedlings ready to go for both the planter and the hanging planters. If you start these seedling batches in a timely fashion, it should be no problem turning over the hanging planters in a few days and getting them set up with new seedlings. When rehanging the planters, take time to meditate on which plants will best integrate with your plant guilds as well as your greenhouse microclimates. Once you have redone and rehung your hanging planters, start another batch of seedlings for midsummer to early fall.

The number of seedlings you should germinate at this time is about half the volume of what you did in winter, as you will require less during the prime growing of summertime. The seedlings started after the hanging planters are hung in the spring are to fill in for any plants that get taken out earlier than the next big overhaul in the fall. In the late winter, you may opt to start some single-harvest crops for the hanging planters, like beets. Once these are harvested, the coverage seedlings work great to squeeze in another round of summer crops before switching to cooler season ones.

Depending on the size and age of the seedlings you transplant into the hanging planters, you will need to consider supplying them with some fertilization to support healthy biomass production. Once the plants are mature enough, a good expectation for feeding frequency is once biweekly; for plain watering, at least once weekly.

Some people will opt for a diverse, nutrient-rich potting mix, which greatly reduces the need for extra fertilization. Others may rely heavily on liquid fertilization, because of a more neutral potting mix blend. The greenhouse manager will need to experiment with fertilization and potting mix type to figure out a system that works well. How you end up doing this is a personal preference.

As spring moves into summer, longer periods of ventilation will be in order, as well as more frequent hose downs and top watering. The overall health of your greenhouse should continue to be monitored. Allow the plants to dictate when they need extra fertilization. Every year will be different, depending on the weather and age of your greenhouse, making it important to take the time to tune in and observe what your plants and the environment are telling you. Some years there may be booming growth, because everything is just right and your freshly applied compost was especially potent. In this case, adding extra fertilizers may oversaturate the plants or stress them out. In other years, your greenhouse may be calling out for lots of heavy feeding or the environmental conditions do not line up well for big growth, so a very minimal amount of extra fertilization is needed. Knowing what is appropriate at different times and seasons is a skill that develops over time.

Summer is not a time for another overhaul of the hanging buckets, because many of the planters you redid in the spring will be in full swing and highly productive. You will have to redo a few planters here and there as needed. Whether or not you redo a planter in the summer depends on the life cycle of the plant and its overall vigor. Robust plants can be cared for until they slow down, most likely well into the fall. It is important to keep in mind that the next full reset of the hanging planters will need to happen in the fall, before winter begins.

The hanging planters, as well as any annuals you planted, need to have a close eye kept on them. When harvesting or watering in the greenhouse, you should always take an extra few minutes to closely examine under leaves and on the stems of your plants. It is very easy, at first glance, to miss some emerging pests, and before you know it, their numbers could swell, catching you off guard. You will be surprised at what you notice when you slow down for a moment and look closely. Make it a point to do regular sweeps throughout your greenhouse pruning and collecting any decaying plant material. Always remember in a no-mulch system to keep it as clean as possible! It requires steady grooming with good technique to thrive. Your main jobs during the summertime are consistent pruning and harvesting, regulating temperature with airflow, and being diligent with top watering as needed. If you have weathered the winter and spring and staged well for the summer, it can be the most fun and rewarding time of year.

If your compost piles have been breaking down and processing well from spring, during the mid to late summer is another great opportunity for a second application of cured compost. This may fluctuate from year to year, so do not worry if the compost piles need more time. Just make sure you are turning out a quality end product, and surely you will have a sufficient batch ready for the fall application. Towards the end of summer, you will need to prepare another large batch of seedlings. The seed selection of this batch should be slower growing, cool season vegetables. Things like greens and some herbs and squashes make good choices as fall and winter approach.

During the summer you may have left the skylights cracked all night. You need to incrementally reduce the duration of time you ventilate the greenhouse each day as you move deeper into fall. Top watering will also slow down progressively. Keep an eye out for any thirsty plants and just water them exclusively with a watering can. It will be helpful to switch to watering plants individually, when and where needed, because as the greenhouse starts to be closed up more often, you need to be careful not to allow too much moisture to build up in the soil and the air. It is easy to overwater in the fall and winter, creating extra humidity, and that can become a breeding ground for mold, and precipitate pest problems or fungal imbalances in the soil. If you check the weather forecast, you may be able to pick a warm, sunny day to do a big watering and hose down of all your plants. If you can get a few of these in before winter, it can greatly help in weathering the congested conditions that will emerge. As stated above, be careful not to overdo. Also, make sure to take advantage of any warmer days that pop up and let the greenhouse breathe as much as possible, which will help buffer the extremes of the coming wintertime.

Once the batch of seedlings started in late summer are a good size for transplanting, it is time to do the second big overhaul of the hanging planters for the year. This should ideally be done by the fall equinox to ensure the plants receive sufficient sunlight hours to grow before the short, dark days of winter set in. Otherwise, you may end up with a flush of smaller, slow-growing plants all winter that will not allow for much grazing or incremental harvesting. At this time you could also cut out any plants that are finished growing and fill in the slot with an extra seedling from this larger batch. If you are in an Earthship that has a double greenhouse, now is a great time to plant greens in the interior planter. As the sun continues to lower in the sky, it will flood deeper into the interior living space, providing a great chance to get a healthy crop of greens going throughout the colder seasons. As a side note, when doing a big overhaul of the hanging planters either in the spring or the fall, it is an opportune chance to clean the inside of your window panes. This is recommended at least once a year, but the more frequent, the better.

Another key task to accomplish during the fall is to spread another round of cured compost onto the topsoil of your garden. When your compost is ready dictates when exactly you do this. If you had a pile that was close to being finished in summer, but not quite ready to be spread out, then you can use that batch to spread into the greenhouse earlier in the fall. If you ended up spreading the second batch of compost into the greenhouse in the summer, then you can wait to apply the third application towards the end of fall. When you spread your compost will change from year to year, and you will have to go with the flow. Sometimes you will get two applications of compost a year, sometimes three or even four in very rare circumstances. Your primary jobs for the fall season are to get the hanging planters up and established before the days get too short, do a thorough compost application onto the topsoil, be judicious with watering, let the greenhouse breathe when you can, and keep everything tidy via good pruning.

Winter is an ideal time to do any heavy pruning and cutbacks on your larger perennial plants. Things like figs or lemon verbena will benefit from this come spring. Normally, during the winter, hanging planters are not redone unless you have a particular plant that is struggling and becoming a pest or disease vector. The days with less sunlight and cooler temperatures slow the plant's activities. So it is better to try and stretch the lifespan of the hanging planters. The plants should be well-established, if planted out early enough, and will provide some steady, yet reduced, yields. Stretching the lifespan of the hanging planters is generally a better option than trying to get young seedlings to maturity during the winter. However, it is wise to get a small batch of cool season seedlings started in the late fall or early winter, just in case you need to take out a plant and require a replacement.

As it gets deeper into winter, continue on the path of reducing top watering and ventilation. It will be rare that you pop open skylights to vent the greenhouse. The cold temperatures outside could quickly damage the plants and knock them out of equilibrium. The winter season is the most heavily altered of the four seasons in the greenhouse. It acts as a kind of extended fall, but with less and less sunlight. It can send mixed signals to the plants, affecting growth patterns and potential vulnerabilities. These aspects play into creating perfect conditions for pests and disease. The extra tools you have at your disposal during the other seasons—like allowing the greenhouse to breathe, soaking down the plants to wash them off, and increased sunlight, helping to bolster plant health—are not available to you, and this can easily tilt the scales into more imbalance. The key to success in the winter is to build a good defensive posture going into it. Once you are in the thick of it, it is time to be both delicate and vigilant with all your maintenance tasks. Water very little, fertilize with discernment, and do not become lax with your pruning regime. If pests and disease do arise, take note of what they are indicating to you and make a plan to correct it in the spring and summer. Good starting points to remedy any issues are incorporating more aerated compost teas to jump-start biological activity and consider adding amendments to your compost to produce a more vibrant end product.

In late winter it is time to get a large batch of seedlings going for the spring redo of the hanging planters, as well as for filling in any open pockets in your greenhouse planter. These seedlings should be warmer season crops, because they will reach maturity in the late spring and summer. Throughout this season, it is best to take a step back, slow down, and try and maintain everything you built up during the year. Take stock of successes and challenges that came up and plan to adjust accordingly. The major duties of the winter entail pruning your larger perennials, doing maintenance gently, making realistic goals for the coming year, and staging well for the spring.

To summarize the major points of a no-mulch greenhouse: consistently maintain and produce quality compost; apply cured compost to the garden at least twice a year; be diligent in pruning and maintenance tasks; clean your windows at least once a year; get big batches of seedlings going in the late winter and late summer to redo all the hanging planters around the equinoxes; take the time to tune into your garden and fertilize when and how best appropriate. The no-mulch greenhouse will require the most attention, but the results can be beautiful and rewarding.

MONO MULCH GREENHOUSE

The mono-mulch greenhouse stands as the median between a no-mulching setup and a poly-mulch greenhouse. This option is not as heavily dependent upon grooming the greenhouse as rigorously and thoroughly as in a no-mulch system, but will still call for more than a poly-mulch operation. The yearly routine is similar to a no-mulching system, but with a few key differences. If you decide to operate your greenhouse in this manner, you will need to decide the frequency of mulch application. There are essentially two options.

First, you could apply the mulch and allow it sufficient time to be broken down to the point that it becomes so bare that the topsoil is showing underneath. The advantage of working on this longer timeline is that, before you reapply a layer of mulch again since the soil is so bare, you could first do a layer of cured compost and then mulch on top of that. This would provide an extra boost to fertility and nutrition for your soil and plants.

In the second method, you could opt to just continually top up your mulch so that no topsoil is ever revealed. The advantage to this is that any compost you generate on site could be used entirely in other forms, such as aerated compost teas, giving you greater flexibility in usage.

So, on one hand, you have a once-a-year to once-every-other-year bigger task, and on the other, you have a seasonal smaller task. Both are viable options and depend on your time and what resources you have available. For example, if you have access to a consistent, reliable, clean, high-quality mulch throughout the year, then doing more frequent top-ups may be the way to go. Or, if you know that every fall some larger trees on your property will be cut down and chipped, giving you ample mulch for the greenhouse, then choosing to make a bigger one-time application may be the best choice. These are just two of many circumstances that could affect how you choose to run a mono-mulch greenhouse.

In the initial establishment of a mono-mulch greenhouse, you must take into account all of your research, observations, and your greenhouse design process before installing the various plant guilds. As always, be aware of proper spacing, anticipating and planning for mature size. Once the core guilds are in, the hanging planters can be set up. They can then be planted out with seedlings, using any excess to fill in any empty spots in the planter.

At this point, one to two inches of your chosen mulch can be spread evenly across the planter bed, making sure to tuck the mulch in underneath any leaves that obscure the stems or trunks of plants. If your mulching substrate is a good food source for saprophytic fungi, like wood chips, you could effectively inoculate your whole planter bed with a particular strain of mushroom of your choosing. If you plan to do that, order some bulk spawn before establishing the bed or at the time of harvesting the mulch material, so that when it comes time to spread it out you could inoculate the whole mulch pile or sprinkle the spawn in with the mulch as you spread it in the greenhouse.

Spring duties entail maintaining and regulating healthy ventilation levels. The duration of ventilation progressively increases as summer approaches and then reduces as the year moves into fall and winter. Pruning and deadheading will still be high on the list of regular maintenance tasks. However, since the soil will be capable of digesting organic material and more decomposition, in general, will be taking place within the greenhouse, it does not become as critical an issue for some decaying plant scraps to fall onto the planter bed as it would for a no-mulch operation. So, while it is important to groom your greenhouse, instead of doing numerous laps per week, you could dial it back to once a week, or more in some cases if conditions line up right. This reduction in the frequency of grooming also pairs well with the mulch providing better moisture reten-tion, thereby leading to top watering less often. This manage-ment style inherently has more durability and independence, allowing for more freedom and flexibility to tend to the garden when you have the time. In a no-mulch style, you may make sev-eral twenty-to-thirty minute visits a week, whereas in a mono-mulch system you could do one visit a week for an hour or so.

The protocol is the same for hanging planters as with the no-mulch system. In late winter, a large batch of seedlings are prepared and, around the equinox, a full reset of the hanging planters. As noted before, now is a good time to give your win-dows a cleaning up. Once the hanging planters are back up, another small batch of seedlings is propagated in case of plant failures. As spring moves into summer, the hanging planters will need to be monitored and provided fertilization as needed. Towards late spring, instead of applying a layer of cured com-post to the topsoil, this is a good time to top mulch if you are doing a more frequent mulching method, and do a foliar and soil drench application of a freshly brewed aerated compost tea. The application of either of these will help prime the system for the summer growing season.

In the summer, the same things apply. Ventilation is a high priority, as well as providing some hose downs for the plants. Before watering the planter, scrap aside some mulch and make sure that the topsoil is not too saturated underneath. Too much water can cause root rot, fungal imbalances, and spread disease. In the heat of summer, the hanging planters will need more attention than the planter in terms of watering. Mulching the hanging planters is an alternative to stretch the time between mandatory visits and will help better match up the days and times when you have the bulk of your maintenance duties, so you do not make unnecessary trips. Even with some mulch top dressed on the hanging planters, you will need to keep an eye out for droopy plants and spot water them. Since this system does not rely heavily on the application of cured compost onto the topsoil, applying compost teas and other brews can be used as a substitute form of nutrition. The frequency of the application again depends on the conditions of the year and the age of your plants. In late summer a big batch of seedlings is started in preparation for the fall equinox hanging planter overhaul.

With the cooler temperatures setting in, the greenhouse manager needs to be aware and adapt to the changing water and ventilation needs. If your planter requires any liberal waterings during the fall, it can be combined with or replaced by some form of liquid fertilization. Merging fertilization with watering at this time will help fill in the gap that emerges from not applying a layer of cured compost to the topsoil. Once the seedlings are ready, spend a day redoing the hanging planters. Take any opportunities you have to open up the greenhouse on warmer days to help air everything out before the closed up confines of winter begin.

As with the rest of the seasons, winter in a mono-mulch greenhouse mirrors a very similar regimen as in a no-mulch system. It is a period of minimal harvesting and basic upkeep, just biding time to stage up for the new growth of spring. Water on an individual needs basis, and avoid a complete soak down of the planter. If you need to redo or replace any plants in the garden or hanging planters, use any leftover coverage seedlings that are still being nursed to fill in. Take the slower pace of the wintertime to prune back any larger perennials, shaping them well to fit into the space. As spring approaches, it will again be time to plant another set of seedlings for the next wave of hanging planters, around the equinox.

Because there is a significant reduction on the demands of time and attention from the greenhouse manager, compared to the no-mulch method, this style will be the most common and suitable way of managing a holistic indoor garden. Mono-mulching, in some form, is the most balanced approach and is ideal for beginners and advanced alike. The flexibility, resilience, and output gained by working with a greenhouse this way is effective and rewarding for most greenhouse managers.

POLY MULCH GREENHOUSE

The poly-mulch greenhouse system will not be for everyone, but is a dynamic and productive means of management. This style has the most decomposition taking place, which allows for the most flexibility as far as time and energy demands. If you want to keep the aerial parts of your plants very tidy, you can with this system. But, you do not have to because the majority of plants will get chopped and dropped right onto the topsoil of the planter bed once they reach the flowering stage. If you choose to keep the plants well groomed, just cut the clippings and let them fall directly onto the mulch in the planter instead of taking them out to an external compost bin. Do bear in mind that, even if you choose to keep the plants well groomed, there will still be periods of empty pockets in the planter as the next round of cover crops germinate and grow. Empty periods or sections of the planter may or may not appeal to some people.

The advantage to this style is that by using a rotation of cover crops, you generate and retain lots of nutrition within the system, and also create your compost in the planter itself through the perpetual mulching process. In addition to reducing grooming and maintenance demands in the greenhouse, this style eliminates the need for making a larger composting system outside of the greenhouse, saving you even more time. The ideal compost setup to use in conjunction with a poly-mulch operation is a worm bin, sized appropriately to the volume of kitchen scraps typically generated on the site. For hanging planters, management conforms to the same fashion as the other two management styles.

In the spring, either the whole planter or the areas dedicated as cover crop zones get broadcasted out at appropriate rates with a warm-season cover crop blend, and the seeds then gently worked into the soil by hand. Broadcast rates will vary, depending on the blend. A good rough estimate is about one pound of seed to cover 200 to 300 square feet. Most greenhouses fall somewhere in that range, making the use of cover crops very affordable, even if you purchase blends online instead of making your own.

Once they are worked into the soil, for the next few weeks during germination, you need to ensure that the planter bed receives the equivalent of at least one inch of rainfall per week. As long as the compiling of the blend is proper and the correct inoculant is mixed in with the seeds, no extra fertilization will be required, because the crops will be generating what they need and interfacing with each other to reach optimal size and health.

The remainder of spring is for monitoring the plants as they grow, trellising, and training any less-than-ideal formations emerging to make use of the planter space best. For example, some beans can grow quickly and then fall over onto other smaller plants, squelching their growth. In this case, a stake or some string can be used to allow each plant the space and structure it needs to grow properly.

As summer approaches, the cover blend will be much larger and well established. At this point, you have two options for how to manage it. The first method is for faster fertility gains in the greenhouse, and the second is for more overall yields. In the first scenario, you chop and drop all cover crop plants right away, once they begin their flowering period. The reason for this is that once flowering starts, the plants are putting all their energy into flower, fruit, and seed production, with less attention to establishing the root system. This change in metabolism and resource distribution within the plants makes them very susceptible to being fully terminated, with little chance of resprouting from the root. Cutting them down at this stage allows for a clean reset of the planter and for another cover crop blend to be squeezed in during the summer. So, if you choose to terminate your cover blend at the beginning of the flowering period, another warm season blend of seeds will be broadcasted out, worked into the soil, and provided ample watering to assist in germination.

The second option is to let the plants mature and ripen. With cover crop blends that primarily produce edible parts, this can be a great choice for gleaning some unique products from your greenhouse. Tubers, grains, brassicas, and beans are often used in conjunction, so it can be rewarding to get a nice flush of produce while still building fertility. Choosing to allow the cover blend to mature before you cut it down will not always guarantee full termination of every species or plant. Some plants may resprout and grow into the next batch of cover crops. A greenhouse that is operated in more of a poly-culture fashion and on a hobby scale does not have the pressure of needing to produce a cash crop. So, if a plant or two persists into the next round of plantings, it is not as big of a deal as it is in larger scale agriculture, where any stray plants could signifi-cantly impede the volume and quality of subsequent crops. If you decide to let your cover blend mature, harvest each plant at the appropriate time, and then wait until the fall draws closer to completely cut down the whole group of plants for the sec-ond round of planting.

In the first method, when fall arrives, you need to be vigi-lant in cutting down your summer cover crop blend as early as you can once flowering starts. Termination at this time will give the next batch that you broadcast out sufficient time to germinate and produce a solid amount of biomass, before going into the slower growing period of winter. Usually, when broad-casting a cool season blend outdoors, the crop will be winter killed by freezing temperatures, and you need to have the seeds in the ground as early as the start of August to ensure enough biomass production to make it worth it. But, in a greenhouse, you have the advantage of eliminating any chance of frost. So, the fall cover blend can reach the right stage at its own pace, without early frosts threatening to end their life cycle prema-turely.

The same pattern applies in the fall as with spring and

summer. Broadcast the cool season blend, work it into the soil, provide enough water for germination, and then monitor the crops as they grow. In either case of terminating cover blends, during flowering or allowing the crops to fully mature, it is advisable to allow the cool season fall blend to continue to grow throughout the winter, instead of cutting it down and trying to establish another rotation. With the short days and lower ambient temperatures, any blend that is broadcasted out in deep winter would struggle to establish itself and most likely make for a scraggly looking greenhouse until spring comes back around. If you are deliberately allowing your fall blend to mature for harvesting, allow the plants to grow during the winter and wait to chop them down completely until you are ready to broadcast out the spring batch again.

As long as the blends are performing optimally, they require only a minimal amount of extra fertilization throughout the year, if any. Perhaps early on, compost teas could be applied in between chopping down a cover blend and before broadcasting a new one, but as the system matures, it should require fewer and fewer outside sources of fertilization. In contrast to the other management styles, where winter is a poor time to apply much fertilization, in this method, it is the best time to provide some biological stimulus via aerated compost teas. Once you cut down the cool season blend, an application of a hearty batch can go onto the thick mulch layer you have developed over the year. The compost tea will give a significant boost to the soil community and help accelerate the composting and digestion process of the organic material in the planter, as everything gets ready to ramp back up in the spring.

In a poly-mulch management style, worm bins are excellent for helping to make a closed loop system, where all the nutrients and waste get captured and recycled efficiently. Worm teas can be made throughout the year to support any hanging planters you have. If you are mixing in larger perennial plants with your cover crop system, the worm castings can be applied topically on the soil to bolster any nutritional gaps.

Moreover, the one big compost tea that is made for the year, once your system is well developed, can use the worm castings as the base.

As you gain familiarity with how the poly-mulching system works in your greenhouse, you will know best when to broadcast, terminate, or harvest. Over time, you may develop a unique rhythm that caters to the specialties of your climate and seasons. It may be that a combination of terminating one group at flowering and letting another go to seed will suit your needs better than strictly adhering to one way or the other.

As you can tell, this method is very different from the conventional mode of greenhouse management, but holds a lot of potential for diversity of yields, as well as systemic autonomy. For those looking for a fresh new way to work with the greenhouse, that has strong roots in biomimicry and ecologically friendly principles, do not be afraid to give this a try. There is lots of flexibility and it is very fun to grow such a wide variety of plants every year. What this management style boils down to is building good cover blends that suit your greenhouse, and knowing when to terminate your plants to keep the system running smoothly and effectively.

APPENDIX

ACKNOWLEDGMENTS

I want to extend an exceptional thank you to the people in my life that made this book possible. First and foremost, to my Wife Ashley, my Mom Miriam, and my Aunt Ruth for all their support both in the early stages and then financially to help get the book launched. Next, I would like to say thank you to Michelle Lochner, who taught me so much and provided a one of a kind opportunity at Earthship Biotecture, where I was able to pursue my passion and interests on a professional level. I will be forever grateful for the time spent working with the plants in all the Earthship greenhouses throughout the years. Also, a warm and appreciative thank you to the current Earthship staff involved in making my book available to the public. Thank you, Heidi, Lauren, Michelle, Agatha, and Andressa for your flexibility and encouraging attitude towards this project and in making this book a reality.

HELPFUL LINKS

ARS Corporation (arscorporation.jp): After using many different small bypass pruners from many different companies, my favorite pair and the one I use for all my fine and precision pruning is model 320B-M Grape Scissors from ARS.

Baker Creek Heirloom Seeds (rareseeds.com): Incredible seed company based out of southern Missouri. I often order seeds from them and have visited their pioneer village. If you ever have the chance it is well worth the stop!

Biodynamic Planting Calendar (rhythmofnature.net/ biodynamic-calendar): A convenient website to check what type of day it may be if you prefer not to order a physical copy of a biodynamic calendar. If you do want a hard copy with some extra info check out this: (steiner.presswarehouse.com/ mariathun.biodynamic.calendar) and/or (stellanatura.com/ use.html) for detailed biodynamic calendars.

Brix Refractometer (agriculturesolutions.com/crop-soil-and-water-testing/refractometers-brix-meters): This is one of many sites where you can purchase a refractometer. There is a variety of styles, but the basic brix 0-32 scale is ideal for greenhouse work.

Compost Thermometer (reotemp.com): This is a link to a high quality compost thermometer to properly monitor your pile as it moves through different composting stages.

Earthship Biotecture (earthship.com): The main website for all things Earthship. You can check out current events, dates for educational programs, book nightly rentals and purchase merchandise.

Felco (felco.com): One of the best blade-based garden tool companies. It is what the professionals use. Buying a mid-sized hand shear and a large lopper will last you many years if well taken care of.

Iphone Clip-on Macro Lens (xenvopro.com): This is an example of a quality lens at a reasonable price. There are many options to suit your budget and needs. You can always opt for a more standard magnifying loupe, which you could find at most local growshops.

Market Gardener Book (themarketgardener.com): This book is an excellent resource for someone looking for a form of gentler and milder tillage for their greenhouse system as opposed to the no-till options presented in this book.

Plants for a Future Database (pfaf.org): A useful resource for researching plants to incorporate into the greenhouse or learn more about the ones you may have.

Solar Aspect Resources (apps.apple.com/lumos-sun-and-moon-tracker) and (suncalc.net): The first link is an app for iOS users. It is very handy and easy to use for tracking the path of the sun at any time of year. The second link can be accessed via the web and has everything you need to gather your solar data.

Solo Backpack Sprayers (us.solo.global): If you plan to do a heavy rotation of aerated compost teas, be sure to buy a model with a diaphragm pump.

GLOSSARY

Actively Aerated Compost Tea: A fertilization and bioremediation technique that focuses on multiplying and supporting aerobic life forms beneficial to plants and soil.

Anecic: A classification of worm that lives within the earth and creates vertical burrows.

Biodynamic: An agricultural movement initiated by Rudolf Steiner which encompasses holistic methodologies.

Biomass: Living matter.

Biomimicry: The practice of emulating natural patterns in any system or design.

Biotype: An observable physiological form found and produced in nature.

Box Trough Planter: A garden bed designed to responsibly dispose of greywater by distributing the water into an in-ground chamber.

Compost: The process in which organic material is converted into humus through biological forces.

Dipper Box: A dosing method for greywater systems to distribute greywater in incremental batches to a planter or greywater zone.

Dosing Siphon: A flow regulation device used in greywater systems to periodically deliver flushes of water to planter beds or greywater distribution zones.

Earthship: A structure comprised of six design elements—passive solar and thermal mass heating and cooling, solar and wind electricity, contained wastewater treatment, water harvesting, building with natural and recycled materials, and integrated food production.

Ecological Succession: A pattern observed in nature to perceptually increase complexity in biological systems.

Endogeic: A classification of worm that lives within the earth and moves laterally through soil horizons.

EPDM: An impermeable rubber liner, common for sealing ponds.

Epigeic: A classification of worm that lives within its food source.

Epigenetics: Developments, changes, or adaptations that take place in biological organisms over time through environmental inputs.

Ethnobotanical: The human usage of plants and the study thereof.

Evapotranspiration Cell: A type of garden planter that contains subsurface water, beneath soil, producing a wicking action which hydrates the soil and plant roots.

Fall: Plumbing vocabulary for the distance water can flow via gravity.

Global Earthship: A sophisticated and high-performing Earthship model incorporating robust systems and components, a double greenhouse, and thermal wrap within the berm.

Greywater: Household laundry, sink, shower, and tub water.

Guild: The deliberate association of different types of plants to produce harmonious beneficial interactions.

Humus: The organic material produced via composting and found as an essential component of healthy soils.

Inflorescence: A group or cluster of flowers on a plant.

Macronutrients: Nutrients required in larger quantities for plant growth and health. Traditionally the macronutrients are identified as N, P, K, Ca, Mg, and S in no particular order.

Microclimate: An area that has unique qualities and characteristics in comparison to its broader surroundings.

Micronutrients: Nutrients required in smaller quantities for plant growth and health. Traditionally the micronutrients are identified as B, Mn, Zn, Co, Mo, Ni, Fe, and Cl in no particular order.

Modular Earthship: The earliest Earthship model—most noted for a single sloped greenhouse and rammed earth tire U-shaped wall.

Mulch Basin Planter: A garden bed designed to responsibly dispose of greywater by distributing the water directly into a sunken mulch layer.

Multi-Species Cover Crop: An agricultural technique involving cropping systems that incorporate a variety of plants to bolster fertility and health during the annual growing cycle.

Mycelium: The vegetative part of mushrooms.

Mycorrhizal: A classification of mushroom that creates a symbiotic bond with living plant roots.

Off-grid: A term to denote no municipal water, power, or utility lines going in or out.

Organic Material: Decaying or decomposed natural compounds.

Package Earthship: An early Earthship model—most noted for the use of exclusively vertical glass for the main greenhouse.

Parasitic: A classification of mushroom that creates a detrimental bond for a host organism.

Permaculture: A principle-based methodology that seeks to create highly efficient self-sustaining ecosystems.

Poly-Culture: Multiple varieties of plants and/or organisms co-existing in a living system.

Rhizosphere: The root zone of plants.

Ruderal Species: Plants that are adapted to be the first to colonize disturbed or damaged landscapes.

Saprophytic: A classification of mushroom that lives in and digests organic material.

Simple Survival Earthship: An economical and modern Earthship model incorporating a sloped kickup double greenhouse —a rebar birdcage dome mounted on rammed earth tires and paired down systems and components.

Subsurface Flow Wetland: A botanical cell layout and design traditionally used for the treatment of wastewater, utilizing gravel and wetland plants.

Sustainability: A term to characterize any practice that is ecologically sound, renewable, repeatable, and earth-friendly.

Thermophilic: Heat loving. The term is used in this book to classify a phase of composting where temperatures reach 113 to 158 degrees Fahrenheit.

Vermiculture: The practice of cultivating and propagating worms for anthropogenic use.

Vertical Flow Mixed Media Wetland: A style of planter bed designed for cleaning effluent, incorporating sand or mulch and multiple aggregate sizes.

Walipini: A style of greenhouse most noted for being partially underground.

Wicking Bed: A style of garden planter that uses subsurface water and temperature differentials to self-moisturize the soil.

Worm Castings: Humus-like excrement produced through the digestive activity of worms.

Worm Leachate: The liquid drainage found at the bottom of a composting worm bin.

ANNOTATED RESOURCES

Andersen, Arden B. 2014. *The Anatomy of Life & Energy in Agriculture*. Acres U.S.A.

A foundational piece for comprehending the mechanics of soil health and ecological wellness. Clear and direct, this work cuts though so much of the agricultural jargon and gets to the point. If you are new to gardening or farming allow this book to be the basis on which you build all your systems.

Bloom, Jessi, et al. 2015. *Practical Permaculture: for Home Landscapes, Your Community, and the Whole Earth*. Timber Press.

A comprehensive and well structured walkthrough on the permaculture design process and worldview. Permaculture tools and principles utilized in conjunction with Earthship greenhouse management are a perfect marriage. This book does a great job at addressing the multifaceted nature and many layers of the permaculture movement.

"Building the Next Generation of Natural Systems for the Treatment of Wastewaters and the Remediation of Degraded Water Bodies." *John Todd Ecological Design*, toddecological.com.

Todd is a master of ecological wastewater treatment systems. While his work is usually done on a scale larger than residen-

tial structures, his designs and knowledge base is well worth researching to help inform Earthship greywater systems.

Cotter, Tradd. 2015. *Organic Mushroom Farming and Mycoremedi-
ation: Simple to Advanced and Experimental Techniques for Indoor
and Outdoor Cultivation*. Chelsea Green Publishing.

Tradd Cotter is an amazing pioneer in the mycological world.
This book equips the greenhouse manager with everything one
needs to know to get started on a mushroom journey, as well as
mature into sophisticated and technical techniques. Not only
an author and educator, he operates a mushroom cultivation
supply company. Be sure to visit mushroommountain.com to
stock up when in need of all things mycelium.

Crawford, Martin, et al. 2016. *Creating a Forest Garden: Working
with Nature to Grow Edible Crops*. Green Books, an Imprint of UIT
Cambridge Ltd.

A fantastic resource for any Earthship greenhouse manager.
This book covers in depth the principles of forest gardening,
stages, and the how-to of installation, and has a large collection
of plant profiles. Particularly useful in the research and design
phase to key out the perfect plants for your greenhouse.

Grotzke, Heinz. 1998. *Biodynamic Greenhouse Management*. Bio-
Dynamic Farming and Gardening Association.

A straightforward presentation on biodynamic means of working in the greenhouse. This book provides many practical tips
and pointers to help frame your greenhouse management style
from a holistic perspective.

Harty Fe´idhlim. 2017. *Permaculture Guide to Reed Beds: Design-*

ing, Building and Planting Your Treatment Wetland System. Permanent Publications.

The contents of this book are very well synthesized and easy to understand, making wetland systems more accessible to beginners. Moreover the knowledge and experience shared in the book makes this a valuable resource for anyone looking to manage wastewater. Also, check out the website wetlandsystems.ie for more information.

Ingham, Elaine, et al. 2000. *Soil Biology Primer.* Soil and Water Conservation Society, in cooperation with the USDA Natural Resources Conservation Service.

Whether a digital or hard copy, this book belongs in every greenhouse manager's library. The contents shed light on the complex, integrated, and dynamic workings of the soil food web, illuminating the ever-present need to remain grounded in holistic techniques in order to preserve health. Elaine Ingham is a voice in the wilderness and has become a world leader in the agricultural sphere. She provides high quality resources and educational courses. Visit soilfoodweb.com to see her offerings.

Jacke, Dave, and Eric Toensmeier. 2008. *Edible Forest Gardens.* Chelsea Green.

A permaculture classic. The contents and practices of this book synergize seamlessly into a holistic home greenhouse style. This book will deepen your understanding of the niche functions plants can provide as well as how to best utilize them in your system.

Jenkins, Joseph. 2005. *The Humanure Handbook: A Guide to Composting Human Manure.* Jenkins Pub.

More than just a book on composting human waste, it provides a clear presentation on the mechanics of composting itself. A very viable alternative to flush toilets that can produce a quality end product.

livingwebfarms. *YouTube*, YouTube, youtube.com/channel/ livingwebfarms.

This channel has a plethora of educational videos covering a wide range of topics. The cover crop videos are especially informative for understanding and building blends for a poly-mulch greenhouse.

Ludwig, Art. 2014. *The New Create an Oasis with Greywater*. Oasis Design.

Art Ludwig is one of the world leaders on all things greywater. His website oasisdesign.net provides lots of valuable information for free. It is highly recommended for anyone working with any form of greywater system to familiarize yourself with his materials. His books span everything from greywater fundamentals, principles, and mechanics, as well as system styles and even specifics for builders.

Managing Cover Crops Profitably. 2012. Sustainable Agriculture Network.

An excellent resource, particularly for a greenhouse manager who operates a poly-mulching system. Print copies cost from $20 to $30, while the ebook version can be download for free at sare.org/Learning-Center/Books/Managing-Cover-Crops-Profitably-3rd-Edition

Minnich, Jerry, and Marjorie Hunt. 1979. *The Rodale Guide to*

Composting. Rodale Press.

Some cultural information is a bit dated, but all the information on composting is superb. This is an ideal resource to get acquainted with the wide world of composting.

Mollison, Bill, and Andrew Jeeves. 2014. *Permaculture: a Designers Manual*. Tagari Publications.

The definitive guide on all things permaculture. Well worth the investment to help facilitate your permaculture journey.

Morel, Antoine, and Stefan Diener. 2006. *Greywater Management in Low and Middle-Income Countries: Review of Different Treatment Systems for Households or Neighbourhoods*. Sandec at Eawag.

A thorough examination of greywater mechanics as well as a good manual on low-tech designs that could conform for greenhouse use.

Pfeiffer, Ehrenfried. 2002. *Using the Biodynamic Compost Preparations and Sprays in Garden, Orchard, and Farm*. Bio-Dynamic Farming and Gardening Association.

A concise explanation of biodynamic methods. Studied in conjunction with Steiner's lecture series on agriculture and Christian von Wistinghausen's book (see below), it will equip you with everything you need to begin incorporating biodynamic preparations into your practice.

Phillips, Michael. 2012. *The Holistic Orchard: Tree Fruits and Berries the Biological Way*. Chelsea Green.

A great resource on many levels. Not all the information is applicable in greenhouse management, but his fertilization protocols and overall methodologies blend well with Earth-ship greenhouse systems.

Steiner, Rudolf. 2004. *Agriculture Course: the Birth of Biodynamic Method: Eight Lectures given in Koberwitz, Silesia, between 7 and 16 June 1924.* Rudolf Steiner Press.

Can be read for free online at wn.rsarchive.org/Lectures and also downloaded as audio for free at rudolfsteineraudio.com/agriculture

Tichavský, Radko. 2018. *Organon de la Holohomeopatía: Ciencia de la Agricultura para la Vida.* Instituto Comenius.

Physical copies must be purchased through the college itself at comenius.edu.mx/

Wistinghausen, Christian von. 2003. *The Biodynamic Spray and Compost Preparations: Directions for Use.* Biodynamic Agricultural Association.

Informative and practical. This is a great starting point for biodynamics and handy to have as a reference when needed.

ABOUT THE AUTHOR

Daniel Dynan is a holistic farm and garden consultant and permaculture designer. His career started by studying Homeopathy and from there moved into sustainable housing and gardening. Daniel acquired his permaculture designer certificate through Oregon State University. He has also studied Agrohomeopathy, which focuses on the use of homeopathic techniques and remedies for plant systems through Instituto Comenius. During Dan's employment at Earthship Biotecture, he helped formulate the management styles and practices outlined in this book. Scythe & Seed, his design company, is working on supplying educational tools  and resources for beginner and advanced gardeners alike. Originally from Philadelphia, Pennsylvania, he now resides in Taos, New Mexico, where he enjoys hiking, skiing, and lots of fresh air and sunshine with his family. Check out his website at scytheandseed.com.

Made in the USA
Monee, IL
26 February 2021

61390569R00134